PREGNANCY SURVIVAL GUIDE FOR MEN

First-Time Dad's Handbook. All You Need to Know to be Prepared for the Next 9 Months and Beyond + To Do List for each Trimester Included.

Ethan Crawford

TABLE OF CONTENTS

We invite you to scan this **QR code** using the camera of your phone to access your bonus content:

SCAN THE QR CODE BELOW

You will access to **2 EBOOKS**:

1. **"Positive Discipline Methods"**: Get all the support and guidance you need to be a success at correcting your child

2. **"Build Confidence for Kids"**: Teach your kid who to learn from their mistakes and acknowledge achievements & fears. Why it is important to provide responsibilities

INTRODUCTION

Congratulations! You are about to be a father!

I'm sure all your friends and family are giving you big slaps on the back and telling you what good news this is. I'm sure you are already hearing so much advice about what awaits you once the baby comes and what you can expect as a dad.

Take your time and absorb all of the good will, the positive words of encouragement, and the thoughts and prayers that are headed your way. Not to put it too lightly, but your life is about to change forever and you only have nine months to prepare for that!

Does that seem like an overly dramatic thing to say? Well, it is true!

In nine months, you are going to be helping take care of a brand new human being. Whether you are scared, nervous, curious or confident, you are undoubtedly feeling some very strong new emotions around this next great adventure in your life.

You may be asking yourself, what can I do to get ready? Even if you aren't the planning type, I'd be willing to wager that you might think it is worthwhile to start planning for a baby. Why would I be willing to bet that? Simple. You picked up this book!

Your partner has probably already bought a book or ten and might have been bugging you to get a book too. Women have so many pregnancy and birth books, even the most voracious reader would have trouble getting through all of their recommendations within the nine months they have available to them.

But what about dads? What about you? What about what you need to prepare for in the next nine months? What about some really hard lessons about fatherhood that might be sugarcoated by well-meaning friends and family? What about some honest reflections on how things have changed with your pregnant partner and what you can expect during these volatile times? What about getting your house ready, getting your budget ready, getting your body—yes, your body dad!—ready for what is to come.

It can be a lot. But you are not alone.

How do I know all this? What makes me qualified to share this with you? Well, I'm a writer and a father of four from Boston. I know from experience just how challenging pregnancy can be for new fathers and I know that there aren't always spaces and resources for dads the way there are for moms. It's great that moms have so much that they can utilize during this pregnancy time, but I always wished there were more options for dads!

Ten years ago, I felt just like you. I was overjoyed at the thought of my first baby on the way! Also, I was absolutely terrified, horribly uncertain, and wildly insecure about my ability to rise to the challenges of fatherhood.

Here's a little secret I wish I knew then: when it comes to fatherhood, there is no such thing as being "a natural." Some of the greatest fathers start out feeling lost and not ready for the biggest job of their lives. But they learned over time and you will too. All you need is hard work, honesty, and reliable resources to reach for whenever you need a little extra help and guidance along the way.

My book is designed to be a part of what will hopefully be a lot of resources for you as a new father. Hopefully these books will serve as a map, compass, and a companion all at once.

This particular book is here to help and offer you a Pregnancy Survival Guide for dads. Inside you'll find all the tips and tricks as well as universally proven strategies for navigating pregnancy as a man and preparing for a new baby. You'll learn the advice I wish I had ten years ago to hopefully help you navigate with fewer mistakes (or at least shorter recovery times) than I had when I went through this.

You'll also get emotional support that you may be too proud to ask for. It can be hard for dads, or men in general, to be honest, about what their emotional needs are, but it is okay to admit that you may need a shoulder to lean on during the difficulty of pregnancy.

Whether you've had the best relationship with your father or not, it is never too late to embody the fatherhood that you want, one that is positive and filled with love. This is exactly what this book is for.

Together, we will look at all of what you can expect over the next nine months and how you can make it through with the ease of an expert, even if this is your very first kid. We'll also share some real-life examples and stories that my friends and I have collected among our many years of fatherhood trials and errors.

Okay, so the good news is that you have a little bit of time to prepare. But how to prioritize what you're doing? Not to worry. We have a checklist here for you to be able to follow along with a timeline that makes sense over the next nine months as you prepare for fatherhood.

And anyway, you're needing to be ready not just for the pregnancy but for the first few months of your child's life! This wouldn't make sense if you were just getting through the pregnancy. This is all about what to be ready for when it comes to the actual baby being in your living space with you.

All this is to say that this book has you covered. We aren't going to leave you hanging, and we'll have everything clear and laid out for you so that you can be ready every step of the way.

So, buckle the car seat into the holes and hooks you never knew were in your car, and let's get ready to thrive in this pregnancy!

Chapter 1

WE'RE PREGNANT!

Sharing the Good News:

At some point you probably took an at home test. You'll head to the doctor with your partner and get the "real deal" where they will confirm you are expecting. What an exciting day! It is totally okay to be excited and want to shout from a rooftop (or a mountain top if you're out in nature, I don't really know, I'm a Boston boy!) about how thrilled you are that you're about to become a dad!

You'll need to talk through with your partner about how and when you want to start telling people. Maybe you want to share it on social media? It is up to you, but I'd encourage you to take the time to have more personal conversations with people before sharing broadly on social media. It is a special time to be able to talk with your closest friends and family to share this celebration. If it is at all possible, you'll want to see the joy on their faces as you share this life-changing news with them!

Oftentimes, people will decide to wait to share the news until after the first trimester (3 months). The reason why people do that is because they want to wait until there is a better chance of the baby continuing to grow and develop all the way to birth. The first trimesters see the most miscarriages and accidents that can lead to a termination of the pregnancy. It can be hard to share the great joy of pregnancy only to turn around and let everyone know the incredibly difficult pain and feelings of loss that can come with a miscarriage.

My wife and I waited until after the first trimester to tell people. When we talked through it, my wife shared that it was important to her to feel confident in it really happening and (as much as possible) didn't want to have to tell people the painful news of a miscarriage if it were to happen. My wife is a very private person and deals with hard things on her own. It made sense for us to wait until the first trimester was over to share the news.

When my brother and his wife got pregnant, they decided to tell everyone right away. It was Christmas time, and I assumed he wanted to tell us just because the whole family was together and it was a chance for them to share the great news with all of us all at once. Their due date was in August, so there was no way that their first trimester had come and gone. When I asked him about that choice to share the news before the first trimester, he said simply, "These are the people I love! I want to celebrate with them. And I know that if something happens to this pregnancy, I'll be very very sad and these will be the people I will want to mourn with." For him and his wife, it made sense not to wait until the first trimester was over to share the news.

You will have to do what is right for you. There is no right or wrong way to go about it. You'll talk with your partner and figure out what your preferences are. You don't want to think about the worst, but sometimes it is best to plan for the worst and hope for the best. Whatever that looks like for you, you should make your decision based on that.

Whenever you're ready, enjoy the moment. It is such a thrilling conversation to share with beloved family and friends the news that you're about to become a dad!

Self-Care

Self-care is hugely important. Let's just jump right in with that and begin there. It may sound cheesy and it may sound dumb, but it isn't. And I guarantee your partner doesn't think it is either. There are a lot of things that are going to be changing very quickly for you from now on. So, prepare yourself as best as you can for constant change. Take care of yourself in the way you best know how. Different people have different things that they need to do, and it is important that you do whatever self-care looks like for you.

That being said, it is immensely important that you communicate with your partner why you are doing what you are doing. For example, if you are someone who finds restoration by going on a four-hour long hike alone, that's great, but your partner may feel as though you are spending more time away from them. If you can, find a way to let them know that you aren't going to be away from them because you don't want to be with them, but because you are needing to do what is important for yourself to be able to prepare for the massive changes that are coming your way.

At the same time, you need to realize that change has already happened. Your partner, whether you've been with them a few weeks or a few years, is going through something they have never done before and they are going to need different things from you than they did prior to pregnancy. If you were more independent before, even if you had been so for years, it will be important to communicate with her about why you are spending time away, whether alone or with friends, and you may need to find ways to "make up for" your absence.

If it is important for you to spend time with your male friends, it is okay to advocate for that and to let your partner know that you want to be with your friends as you prepare for fatherhood. Maybe some of your friends are dads. Maybe you can talk more easily with your guy friends about some of the fears or concerns you may be having about fatherhood. Maybe you just want to spend time with friends and relax and find a way to clear your mind of all that you've been storing up as you prepare to become a parent. Whatever you need, it is okay to do those things and to let your partner know that it is important for you.

Just remember that you may need to spend extra special time or give special gifts to your partner to communicate appreciation and gratitude not only for what she is doing in carrying your child, but in being supportive of your self-care needs during this time. Self-care during this time is a bit of a balancing act between your needs and your partner's needs. It isn't easy to figure out always where your need for self-care ends and your partner's needs for extra care during pregnancy begin.

It is also okay to prioritize your pregnant partner and tell your friends that they may need to be okay with seeing a little less of you, or making it easier for your partner if they come to visit you instead of you meeting out or going to see them.

This will be different for everyone, but no matter what your self-care routine is, it is very important to talk through what it is with your partner so that you are both on the same page.

You'll also need to be aware of your partner's needs during this time.

One good way of doing this is to get into the habit of checking in together, usually in the morning or by lunchtime at the very latest. It is good to be able to say, "What do you need today?" It invites specific answers and gives a specific timeframe. A good response might be, "I need some time away to reconnect with my friends. I'm happy to be here and make sure you have everything you need before I go."

Self-Care Real-Life Scenario:

Adam and Tanya were married for five years before Tanya became pregnant. They were so excited for their upcoming baby, but they seemed to be fighting more than ever. Adam was always away from the house, and Tanya seemed to be clinging to him and demanding all his time and attention. Adam didn't use to spend that much time away and Tanya used to be fine whenever he was away. The only thing that changed was Tanya's pregnancy.

It didn't take long before things came to a head. Adam wanted to go away on a long weekend trip with two of his friends from college. They took the trip every year, and he didn't see why they shouldn't this year. He figured it might be the last year they could take the trip, since he didn't know if it would be possible once he became a dad. When he talked with Tanya about his plans to be gone, she erupted! "You're always gone, you are never here, you want to see your friends more than you want to see me, and I know it is because I'm pregnant and I can't have fun with you anymore! I'm supposed to have you around more than ever but you're never here!"

Adam didn't know what to say. He was shocked. He called his friends and told them he was going to have to put the trip on hold this year. He still wanted to go, but he knew he needed to have more talks with Tanya before he could commit to a weekend away. After a cooling-off period, Adam and Tanya were able to talk through why they both felt the way they did. Adam was nervous about becoming a dad, and it made him feel better to connect with his old friends. Tanya, who normally wouldn't care at all about Adam being gone, felt lonely without him there, and a little resentful that he got to continue living his life with his friends while she had a more limited social life due to her pregnancy.

After some hard conversations, Adam and Tanya were able to agree on the fact that they would have to find a new way forward together. Tanya would tell Adam when she needed him home and Adam would try and do a better job to be present for Tanya in ways that she needed him. The two of them planned their own weekend trip for the next month, and after a special date night, Tanya felt that Adam really was prioritizing her. She encouraged him to go on his trip with his friends, as long as he promised to call every night he was away. Adam happily agreed, and they were able to both have a smoother pregnancy experience moving forward.

We're Pregnant Summary:

You're about to go through something you've never gone through before. So is your partner. As you figure out what you need during this time, be sure to communicate what those needs are and be receptive to what your pregnant partner needs as well. Find ways to come to terms with the fact that you are no longer going to be able to do all that you want to do with the same level of freedom that you used to. But that doesn't mean that you have to completely abandon everything you did and your whole sense of self. This will just take some time and intentionality to figure out new ways to live into what self-care means for you.

Be ready to make changes that benefit your pregnant partner. They are really going to need you to show up in different and maybe some unexpected ways. Don't be afraid or ashamed to communicate with them in new ways to make sure you are able to be present for them in whatever way they are needing now.

Chapter 2
FIRST TIME DAD 101

There are many questions that fathers-to-be will immediately have after finding out their partner is pregnant. You probably have your head swirling with so many thoughts and questions, and I hope to be able to offer some responses in this chapter.

Sex During Pregnancy:

Let us just start out by saying that it is okay to have sex during pregnancy. In fact, your partner has an increased sex drive during pregnancy due to certain hormonal changes.

That being said, your partner may also go through fluctuating feelings about her body and her comfort level with it. Essentially, you should not be surprised to see a more sporadic sex life than you may be accustomed to in your relationship.

Chances are you may have times with increased sexual frequency and other times of almost no sexual contact. Be sure that you are communicating with your partner and really listening to their needs around sex during the next nine months.

Relationship Changes During Pregnancy:

Everything is going to change during pregnancy, which includes your relationship. You do not have to worry though, not all changes are bad changes. In fact, this is an opportunity for you two to have a shared experience that you've never had before. If you really focus on your communication, you can grow deeper in your relationship and come out stronger through the course of the pregnancy.

Some things will never be the same, however, and it is helpful if you know that. A lot of the routines that you may have built up during the time you've been together will probably change. Maybe they will change for health reasons or due to general shifts in your partner's mood or desire to engage in activities.

It is best if you can be flexible and again—I hate to sound like a broken record here—be sure to be communicating with your partner about what these changes feel like for you and what your needs are during this time of great change.

Finances:

Things are about to change for you. Even if you got a lot of the things on your baby shower wish list and even if you've been financially secure for a while now, having a baby changes everything. You'll need to take a look at how the baby impacts your budget and what this means for the rest of your finances.

Please have an honest conversation with your partner about what makes sense for your new family. You may be surprised at some expenses, and that includes hospital bills that accompany the birth. It depends on your insurance, so I don't want to say what exactly you should expect, but you should expect a bill in the mail.

Clothes, shoes, diapers, new toys, bigger car seats and strollers, bigger cribs, all come and go in the first year. It is going to be something that you'll need to figure out how you are paying for it. Even if you are using second-hand stores, hand-me-downs from family and friends, and a lot of economical ways to make things work, you are still going through a big financial change.

This is not to mention childcare costs. If your partner has a good maternity leave, she might get three months off from work. Maybe you get a month? (For the record, Europe, Canada, Eastern Asia, basically the whole developed world does parental leave so much better than we do it is pathetic).

Is your partner planning to not work and be a stay-at-home mom? Do you have family wanting or willing to help with childcare? Or are you ready to start paying for childcare five days a week for the next few years until they are in school? Maybe you want to hire a nanny who can come to your house? Or maybe you have a particular daycare you really love because you've done your research and you believe in their educational philosophy for teaching colors and shapes. Regardless, if you're paying for childcare, you can expect to spend at least $20,000 per year per kid. If you are in certain parts of the country, that number will be laughably small. My friends George and Cory live near San Francisco and pay nearly $65,000 per year for their two kids to have a nanny.

The point is that having a kid dramatically affects your budget and you need to talk with your partner about it.

First Time Dad 101 Summary:

You're going to be a great dad, but it will be helpful to have a good community of dads surrounding you. Don't be afraid to have sex during the pregnancy, but be ready for your partner's shifting moods. There are going to be a lot of shifts over the next nine months, but if you work really hard, you and your partner can come out stronger. Be sure you are addressing your finances now, as that will impact a lot of what you end up doing over the course of the pregnancy.

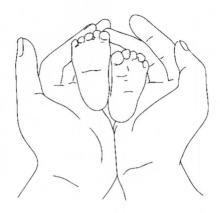

Chapter 3

THE FIRST TRIMESTER

T he baby will start developing its brain and spinal cord. At the end of the first month, it's about the size of a grain of rice, but by the end of the first trimester, it's grown into a fetus.

The First Trimester:

We already talked a bit about the first trimester (months 1-3), but there is a lot more to know before you head into it. In the first place, let's look at what determines the dates we're about to be locked in on for the next nine months. The due date and gestational period are determined as being nine months after your partner's last period. It doesn't matter when conception happened. It counts back to her last period and you go from there. I was shocked when I learned this.

My good friend Jon travels a lot with his job and he was out of the country for a while on a work assignment. When he got back, he and his wife continued trying and ended up conceiving! It was great! Until they went to the doctor and he shared the due date. Jon did some mental math and got confused. "But that means... hey I was out of the country then!"

The doctor looked mortified and quickly started to explain and reassure Jon, "No no! It's just an estimation and it is based on her last period, you can definitely be the father of this child!"

Jon's wife, Julie, just rolled her eyes and laughed. "He knows, Doc. He's trying to be funny. He read all about the conception timeline and I think he just wanted to get a reaction out of you."

"I'd say it worked!" Jon said, smiling.

I never heard if the doctor smiled or laughed.

At any rate, just so you don't get surprised, the timeline starts when your partner's last period was. So, if you were out of the country, don't worry. Odds are, you're still the dad!

For your partner, the first few weeks may not seem very different from normal life. Depending on when you found out you were pregnant, it may be a while before there are many changes that you can observe.

The first trimester will happen without a lot of physical changes on the outside from your baby's mother. You may not be able to see much on the outside, but it will be very clear to her internally that things are changing. This is most often when women experience morning sickness and nausea. My partner never actually got sick, but said it felt like non-stop car-sickness for three months.

This is also the time when cravings will start. They can start as early as five weeks in, so be ready for some really absurd food requests. With our second child, my wife wanted lemon and dill added to the grilled cheese. Not only did she want that particular food, but she wanted to continue her independence and wanted to make dinner herself. Not only did she want to make dinner herself, but she very thoughtfully wanted to make dinner for me. Knowing that I typically had a larger appetite than she did, she made me four lemon and dill grilled cheese sandwiches because she wanted three for herself and didn't want me to miss out on this delicious culinary treat. I did my best. You do yours.

As much as you can, try and anticipate those cravings. If she starts wanting gummy worms, keep a big bag in the pantry. If she loves a certain kind of chip, bring home extra from the store. It'll save you trips, her aggravation, and you all will get along a little bit better.

Be in conversation with your partner about what it is that they need. Don't be surprised if there are mood swings. Do not comment on possible mood swings.

Seriously, your partner's hormones are going to be doing absolutely batty things that they've never done before and their body won't really know what to expect or how to handle it. There is a good chance it can manifest in some pretty outlandish emotional outbursts. And that is okay. Be gracious and remember that this is temporary.

They may be tired a lot of the time too. I mean, their body has just accepted another life that is doubling and tripling in size every few days. Their organs are going to be shifting around and contracting and expanding to make room for this child. It is a bodily transformation that you or I could never fully comprehend. Unless you're a doctor or something, but I'm betting if you're reading this book, you're probably not an OBGYN. No offense.

You will, however, have to see the OBGYN quite a lot over the next few months. So, get used to heading to the hospital. Before you ask, yes, you do need to go. Technically, you aren't being evaluated medically, and there is nothing much for you to do for most of the time, and a lot of what is being shared won't mean that much to you, but it is still important that you go to be there with your partner through it all.

It is also great to be an informed dad. This habit starts now. You don't want to wind up not knowing your child's teachers, clothing sizes, or best friends. You are already practicing fatherhood and you are showing your child that you are wanting to be present to know everything about them from the first possible moment.

The first visit to the doctor is the longest. They do a much more involved physical on your partner during that visit. The rest of the first trimester is more along the lines of just checking in to make sure everything is progressing as it should be. You'll be visiting the doctor every four weeks (about once a month) for the rest of the first trimester. It will feel fairly standard with blood pressure and weight being observed. Sometimes other blood tests may be necessary, but early on, there isn't much to do or see.

Around week 9 or 10 (or whichever visit is closest to 9 or 10), you'll probably hear a fetal heartbeat with a cool machine called a doppler. They do have doppler machines that you can buy and have at home. It's up to you if you choose to keep one around. Some partners find it reassuring to be able to check in on their little one's heartbeat from time to time.

Other times, it can become a bit obsessive and unhealthy for you or your partner to spend too much time trying to locate the heartbeat. Often people who struggle with managing their anxiety, need to make the wise decision to leave the heartbeat monitoring to the professionals in the doctor's office and leave the home checkups alone by not ordering a home doppler.

Around week 11 or 12, there may be an ultrasound scheduled. This is probably the first time you get that little picture that looks what you think an ultrasound looks like. It's the little black unrolled cone shape and there is a little bean there and maybe your doctor has technology enough to draw an arrow and add some text that says "baby!" or "head!" This happened on our last child, and my wife was so sad that it ruined the continuity of the other text-less ultrasound pictures we have of our other three children.

It is okay to tell your doctor that you do not want text drawn on your ultrasound. You need to practice advocating for your wife's wants, even (and perhaps especially) in the medical setting, so you might as well get started now.

How to Help:

In the first trimester, it is good to establish the groundwork that you'll build off of for the next six months leading up to the birth. Start really talking with your partner about making sure their needs are met and yours are too.

I don't mean to assume that you and your partner fall into traditional gender norms, but I will say that this is the phase when most men need to be encouraged to do a little more around the house. Again, only do so if your partner finds it helpful and if it is something that is comforting for her. Remember, my wife wanted to make dinner a lot, especially after she tried my cooking.

Still, it might be nice to offer to make meals, clean up around the house, start doing more laundry. It may seem small, or it may seem trivial, but I guarantee you that in a couple of months, those little tasks around the house will become next to impossible for your baby's mother to do on their own and it will be good if you know how to do them so that you can help when she is unable to.

Be mindful that a lot of little behavioral changes (more than just doing chores around the house) need to start now. If your partner smokes or drinks a lot, you'll need to be a positive and encouraging force for dropping those habits. You'll also need to do more heavy lifting and maybe carrying things for her. Don't be too proud to carry her purse. You'll be amazed at how heavy it is and how she carries it around seemingly effortlessly all the time.

Also, it is good to get in a healthy habit of complimenting your partner. I say it from past experience and trust me when I tell you it will pay off. Find little things that will make them feel extra loved and start doing them. Especially in the next few months, she is going to feel unattractive and sad about weight gain. It may not make sense to you or me, but it is not helpful to say, "You're supposed to gain weight! You're carrying a baby!"

Hopefully, your partner has healthy self-esteem, but I'm telling you that it goes a long way for you to bring flowers, write notes, take them on special dates, or do whatever you know it is that your partner loves to make them feel special, attractive and valued. You may find your partner's sex drive has increased. This is again a "hormonal thing." Please enjoy this aspect of a hormonal thing. You won't enjoy all of the aspects of the "hormonal things" that she is going through and that are about to happen.

It is not uncommon for them to target you with their anger and frustration. Think about every sitcom from the '80s and '90s that you can imagine. "You did this to me!" the woman screams at the man during a hilarious episode where the dad just grimaces and keeps drinking his beer.

It can feel unfair. You both made this decision. You both engaged in practicing the conception. And your body continues to be your own, and hers is starting to be taken over by something that is growing inside of her in a way she cannot control. She's going through a lot. Make her feel special for doing it all for your family.

Looking Ahead:

You think you have a lot of time, but I'm here to tell you that it isn't as much time as you think. Nine months can feel forever away, but there is more to do than you probably realize, and it is good to be ahead of things instead of scrambling at the last minute to get everything ready for the baby.

Start making a list now of all that you need to prepare for. You don't have to necessarily do everything now, but you're going to want to get at least a few of the things started. Remember, you might want to wait until the end of the first trimester to even tell some of your friends and family, so it is okay not to do too much at this early stage.

That being said, this is the most "normal" time of the pregnancy, so it is okay for you to be efficient early on and prioritize what it is that you're needing to do for the next six months.

Oh, and even though I said earlier that viability happens at six months of pregnancy, this book is going to assume you will carry the baby to full term and that you have a full nine months of pregnancy to prepare. It would be a half-assed attempt at a book to stop at six months and tell you, you should be ready. Or I guess it would be more of a two-thirds-ass attempt, but that's the kind of dad joke you really hone in the final trimester, so it is important to keep that option open.

Seriously though, these first three months can be valuable planning time. You can map out what you want the next six months to look like and when you hope to do a lot of the big things that are going to be on your to-do lists moving forward. There will be a checklist at the end of this chapter and one at the end of the next two chapters as well. Feel free to skim ahead, combine checklists, dog-ear pages, whatever you feel you need to do to start your planning.

Now is also a good time to get the baby growing apps. This book isn't going to detail all the changes that your baby is going through at this time. There are so many apps and books on that. If you want an app to compare your child to the size of a fruit or a cute animal or even a toy, there are apps out there for that. I'd recommend the toy one. It gets weird when it goes from a baseball glove to a bowling pin. You know that it means size and not shape, but it is still a jarring alert to get on your phone.

First Trimester Real-Life Scenario:

Brian and Courtney were so excited to finally become pregnant! They had been trying for years and unfortunately had a couple of miscarriages along the way. The grief that accompanied those losses will never totally go away. There is, however, a beautiful and particular joy for them now that they have made it through the 12-week mark and have maintained the pregnancy through the first trimester!

The couple proudly told their friends and family about the pregnancy and were immediately swamped with questions. "Have you picked out a name?" "Do you have any cravings yet?" "Why aren't you showing?" "Does she make you do everything around the house?" "When is the baby shower?" "What's the due date?" "Boy or girl?"

It was a little overwhelming for them at first and after making the rounds to tell their closest loved ones; they sat down one night to talk about all the questions they had heard. Brian, in particular, felt inadequate. "I don't know the answer to almost every question that people ask me," he confessed to Courtney. "I don't know either, but they all seem like really reasonable pregnancy questions. Are we not prepared enough for this?"

Together, they decided to go to a local bookstore and buy a couple of books to help them prepare for the next several months. As they continued to read and meet with their doctors, they came up with a "pregnancy plan" for themselves that they became comfortable with. It helped them to organize their thoughts, map out a timeline for when they would get things done, and made them feel better prepared to answer the questions that their friends and family may have for them.

As they went through the rest of their pregnancy, it was invaluable to them to have this kind of a roadmap to guide them through the different stages and phases. The whole way along, they knew what to expect, how to talk with their friends, and what they wanted to do moving forward. Even when new or unexpected things came up during the pregnancy, they were equipped and ready to talk through what they wanted and why. They also knew how their decisions would impact future timelines they had already planned out. Because of the hard work they put into the beginning of things, they felt prepared and ready for the challenges of pregnancy all the way up to the birth of their firstborn child.

First Trimester Summary:

You have a lot to learn and a lot you need to talk about with your partner to make sure you're on the same page about things. This will be important because it will set the tone for the entirety of your pregnancy together.

Figure out when you want to tell people. Make sure it feels right for you and your partner both before you start going around having the big talk with your friends and family about your pregnancy.

Start being an involved dad now. Go to the doctor's visits. Ask questions so that you know what they are talking about. Advocate for your partner and be a calming presence in the doctor's office or hospital.

Be ready for a lot of changes in your partner's life and body. As someone who is going to have relatively the same life habits and body for the next several months, be ready to take on more responsibility and be ready to offer more help when it is needed.

Enjoy the hormonal changes when they are in your favor and respond with grace and patience when they are not in your favor.

Start planning ahead for all that you will need to be ready for in the coming months. You'll be glad you did!

First Trimester Check List:

- [ ] Get a positive pregnancy test

- [ ] Schedule doctor's visit to follow up on pregnancy test and confirm she is pregnant (I know these are easy ones to start off with, but there are going to be a lot of blank ones, so these are just going to feel good to check off and make you feel like you've accomplished something!)

- [ ] As the doctor one question (again, this is a motivation for you—you can do it!)

- [ ] Tell your friends and family!

- [ ] Do something special for my partner

- [ ] Eat one food that is clearly a craving food as an act of solidarity with your partner

- [ ] Plan your next several doctor's visit and put them on your calendar

- [ ] Hear the baby's heartbeat

- [ ] See the ultrasound

- [ ] Do something special for my partner

- [ ] Determine what chores I can help out with more
  - [ ] Cleaning
  - [ ] Cooking
  - [ ] Running Errands

☐   Other _____

☐   Start Pregnancy Planning for the next several months

Do something special for my partner (I'm telling you, you're going to want at least three check marks on this checklist. That's just one a month! You know you probably should do special things for your partner more often than once a month. She is carrying your child, after all!).

Chapter 4

THE SECOND TRIMESTER

During the second trimester, your baby will grow from being around 7.5cm, and weighing 30 grams in week 13, to around 23cm and 820 grams at week 26. Your baby will be able to move freely within the amniotic sac in your uterus.

You have made it past the first trimester. Or, at least, you have read past the first trimester. That is good. You are going to want to be prepared for what is coming next. It comes fast and it can be easy to fall behind or, even if you are not behind, it can be easy to feel like you're behind. So, good on you! Keep reading and keep going. You've got this.

The two main parts of this section of the timeline will be the house prep and the second trimester.

Your house (or your apartment or your condo or your cottage or your camper) is no longer your own. I am going to go into detail on all the things you need and all that you do not need and all the things that you are going to get even though you do not need them because they will make your partner happy and that will be worth it in the end. Trust me.

The second trimester is very different from the first trimester. You will notice changes in your partner and there will be new pieces of this that you are going to have to deal with in different ways. Some of it may be downright terrifying. It's okay to be scared. The second trimester is going to have a lot of big decisions for you and this book is here to help you weigh and evaluate those crucial choices so that you can feel equipped to make a well-informed decision with your partner if and when the time comes.

The House Prep:

There is a popular phrase in the UK that says, "A man's house is his castle." You may have heard it even if you live outside of the UK, and I imagine that even now just reading that line inspires you. What man doesn't want his domicile to feel like his castle? Even if you're renting or share a duplex, your space feels uniquely yours and you have possession over it in a way that no one else can ever truly understand.

Chances are you're the one who handles much of the maintenance of your castle. You may do the yardwork, home improvement projects, or any sort of building tasks that may come up in the life of a home. Or hopefully at the very least you remember to change the air filter on your AC unit every six months at the latest. Or at least you make sure your super knows about the leak in your bedroom that seems to become less of a slow leak and more of a slow pour after every thunderstorm that rolls through.

The point is, you have a space that you are the master of. You are going to have to surrender that space. Almost entirely. Guard what you can of it but come to terms with the fact that it is no longer yours. I know that the baby isn't due for another six months, and odds are your partner already has carved out a significant space for themselves and how they envision the pregnancy going, but you need to surrender now.

Do you remember that scene in the *Lion King* when Mufasa takes Simba and says, "Everything the light touches will be yours?" And Simba immediately asks about the one place where the light doesn't touch because that is basically what happens when royalty look out at the expanse of what they have—they notice the one bit they don't own and want to take control of that too?

Where was I? Oh yeah. "Everything the light touches." Soon enough it will be, "Everything the kid touches." And let me assure you, there are no shadowy lands in your home. That kid is going to touch everything. So, get ready now.

A good rule of thumb is if your legs can touch it, so can they. And they'll be able to touch it sooner than you'd think. And you won't want to be drilling and hammering away at things while they're taking a nap once they're born. So, you might as well get everything ready now.

Finish What You Started:

If you have always wanted to have a project done around the house, do it now. If you have always hoped to finish something that you started, do it now. Believe me when I say that there won't be time to do it once the baby is born. Even if there is time to do it, you are not going to want to spend that time doing a home improvement project. You are going to want to spend it with your family, or you're going to want to spend it away from your family but not working.

My friend Zach always wanted to have a kind of a patio in his backyard. His backdoor opened onto a few stairs that went down into the yard and he felt it was a huge missed opportunity for him. One weekend, in a burst of motivation, he tore down the stairs and got rid of them, leaving a giant step down from his back door to the yard.

Zach was never one to finish something that he started. Or at least he wasn't the kind of person who might complete a task in an orderly manner. It would get done eventually, but it would probably require another random burst of energy and an immense amount of boredom coupled with every friend not being available to hang out in order to motivate Zach to actually put a back patio together.

Fortunately for him, he and his long-time girlfriend Katie got pregnant and moved in with him. She did her best to be polite and patient with him, but when the second trimester rolled around and she was still having to take a giant step down or up to get out or in through the back door, she told Zach that she was going to call a handyman to put some stairs in if he didn't get something put together by their next doctor's visit.

Zach, who had no reason to be, was a prideful man. (Please know that I love Zach and I say this in a spirit of good-natured teasing of a friend!).

It hurt Zach to think that a handyman would be called in to do work on his home. So, he called up a few of his friends, yours truly included, and together we were able to draft some plans for a small patio on the back of his house.

It wasn't nearly the large extravagant vision that he had been hoping for, but in two weekends of planning and so many trips to the hardware store, we were able to put together a back patio that had enough room for a table, chairs, and a grill. It had to be a small grill, but there was still enough room.

Katie felt better about stepping up and down to get into and out of the house, Zach improved his home value, and the two found that they enjoyed spending the evenings out back holding their little baby a few months after that patio was built.

Baby Proofing: Adjustments to the Home You Love

There are two main aspects to getting your house ready after you've completed all the unfinished projects that your Katie is going to push you to finish before she gives birth to your child. There is baby proofing and baby prepping. Baby proofing is changing just about everything you have around the house already and baby prepping is adding all the new things to your home that a baby will need. We're going to start with baby proofing.

There are plenty of dedicated professionals at your local hardware store who can guide you to the section that has all the baby proofing that you'll need for your home. Yes, there are aisles for this. You may have walked by them hundreds of times and never noticed because, let's be honest, you've never had to think about baby proofing your home before.

Some of it, you may have expected—those little plastic outlet covers, for example. I hope you expected it. Before you go to the store to get these little devils, make sure you do an accurate inventory and count of all the outlet covers you need in your home. And then buy at least a dozen more than you think you need. Seriously. It will save you a trip to the store later. You can trust me or you can trust your counting and your math skills.

If you trust your math skills, ask yourself if it is worth it to possibly save $5.99 on an extra box of the covers or if you want to spend your afternoon taking another trip to the store. Because you aren't going to be able to convince your partner that they don't all need to be covered, although you may have very good reasoning behind why certain outlets have a lower probability of being touched by your newborn. Buy the extra covers.

You're probably also thinking about those damn little baby-proof latches for every door and drawer in your house. You may think you don't need them for everything. Why, after all, why would the baby go into the small door on the TV stand that has the old DVDs that you still haven't donated to charity yet even though you don't own a DVD player? (This joke assumes a certain age. If all of your movies are on the cloud, or if you've never owned a movie and have had the ability to stream every movie you've ever seen your whole life, good for you. The kid still wants in that door).

I'm going to break some news to you and I'll be as gentle as possible here. Not every door and drawer will accept the same latch. It is going to take some critical thinking on your part to determine what you do and do not need. Hopefully, you can get a more accurate count than you could with the outlet covers, but there is no shame in over-purchasing to save yourself a trip back out just so you can finish one more door.

Obviously, it is up to you what you do or do not want around your house, and you're going to have to face the humiliation of struggling to open your own cabinets for a while, but you need to make it happen. There are a few fancy versions that you can rotate around so that they are not always latching. If possible, I would recommend buying those. I'm not going to shill for any brand or anything like that, but I will tell you that it is helpful, especially if you end up having more than one kid.

Instead of uninstalling and reinstalling them all, you can just flip the latch so that when they're old enough, everyone can open everything easily enough and flip the latch back so that when the next baby comes, you saved yourself a lot of trouble. In our house, we have a sliding drawer for our trash and recycling. The latch gets turned off baby-proof mode when I'm in there cooking dinner and back on to baby-proof mode whenever my youngest is around. It's a good option to have available to you.

Now, we get to the less-thought-of things. Unless you're from the Bay Area or are some sort of "seismophobe" (That's someone who is afraid of earthquakes—didn't know you'd leave a fatherhood book with some bonus trivia knowledge, did you? But there you go. An extra gem just for you) chances are you don't have anything anchored in your house.

Anchor it now. Sing "Anchors Away" if you want while you work on this project, but you need to do it. Anchor your bookcases to the wall especially. And push all your books back as far as you can. And make sure none of the bottom two shelves have any books on them. Get rid of your bookshelves and use your library card more.

If you don't have a stud finder, get one and use it. If you don't have a drill, back way up to before you get your door and drawer latches and make sure you get a drill. Sorry for just assuming you had a drill. Don't borrow your dad's, by the way. Get your own. You'll need it and use it for so many more things that are coming up next in this chapter. Trust me.

In all seriousness, you are going to want to anchor the tall furniture to the wall. A grandfather clock, the chest of drawers in your room, the bookcases that you kept despite me recommending two paragraphs ago that you get rid of them, all of it.

If your TV is mounted on the wall, great. Make sure it is very very secure. Same thing with mirrors and pictures and anything else you have hanging on your walls. I'm not going to tell you about this horror story that my mother-in-law told me about a mirror sliding out of its frame and slicing of a kid's toes because it absolutely traumatized me, even though they reattached the toes and the kid was fine and was so young they may not even remember the incident. I'm definitely not going to tell you that nightmare of a story, though, so don't worry.

Secure everything that needs to be secure.

If you need to get straps to secure your TV to the TV stand, that's okay. Take your time and look at the back of your TV to make sure you have the right sizes for what you need. Some straps will say they're universal. That should work. Still, check your TV first and make sure you're going out to get what you need. Decide if your Xbox needs to be strapped too or if you need to find a way to secure it or keep it out of reach. Tough choices, I know, but you can do it.

Baby Prepping: Something New This Way Comes

The crib. You knew this was coming. But did you also know about the changing table? The new rocker or glider that your partner is going to want in the room for nursing? A new setup in the close to accommodate all the baby clothes and shoes that your partner is going to buy, even though it might be literally impossible for the child to wear that many outfits in the allotted time that they have for that age? I mean if the clothes are for kids age 0-3 months, there are a maximum number of 90 outfits assuming one outfit per day, right? You'll soon learn that your partner isn't going to keep them in one outfit per day. So yeah. You may need to rethink your closet space. The diaper genie? Yeah, even if you are doing cloth diapers (a tough choice we'll go over later) you still need a depository for the diapers.

This section, you definitely want input from your partner on. Chances are she has an idea about what she is looking for in a crib, changing station, and closet set up. She probably also has an idea about the color scheme that you'll need to paint the baby's room. Seriously. Ask her. If you haven't already, she's been begging for you to ask her.

Obviously, the focus is on the baby's room. The first few months the baby should be staying in your room (again, we'll get to some of that a little bit later) but eventually they are going to move into their own room and this is the space you're going to need to have ready.

Take your time, talk with your partner, and make sure you have everything you are going to need. It is up to you, but we went with a crib that could adjust from a very low setting to a very high setting. The crib was also a very tall crib. We did that because both my wife and I are fairly tall, but you will want to make sure you can reach over the top of the crib to get down and pick up the baby without breaking your back. It's a move you're going to have to do a lot of. Especially in the middle of the night. So, it's important to think through what you want in your crib.

Make sure you have enough space in the room for the crib. Get it early and build it early. Put it in there early and make sure it is good to go. You don't want to be building it a month before the baby is due, only to have your partner go into early labor and you have a half-built crib at home when you rush off to the hospital.

Put the changing station next to the crib. I don't care if that messes up the vibe of the room or if it feels weird with where the window is. You do not want to be carrying the baby all around back and forth between the crib and the changing table. You want to minimize the time you are holding the baby when they need a diaper change. For both of your sakes.

Make sure the station you choose has everything you need. Space for diapers. Space for wipes. New clothes. New sheets. Probably some new space for the other things you didn't think of yet but will pop up in time. Again, choose a station that makes sense for your height. Don't break your back every time you have a diaper change and down reach up into the heavens either. Make it just right for you, Goldilocks.

Build the glider or buy it, but make sure it is what your partner likes. And bring WD40 to have nearby. Don't say anything to your wife about it. It has nothing to do with her weight, but a lot of gliders will squeak after the constant use they get. Your partner may never had needed a chair so much, especially if that becomes the spot where they do a lot of breastfeeding (It is okay if they don't do a ton of breastfeeding too, and you may do some formula feeding yourself in that chair, bub). At any rate, you want it to glide smoothly and silently and you don't want your partner concerned about their weight gain and if that's making the chair squeak. Just spray the WD40 on all the joints if you start to hear it squeak.

Also, this may be a personal preference thing, but our child really slept much better on their own (naps and overnight) when we got them blackout curtains for their room. The curtains helped with sound as well as light, and things went much better for their sleep schedule after we installed them. Of course, that was part of the rough learning on the first kid, and things went much better for the subsequent three. Still, it's probably a good idea for you to get the curtains. Not a requirement like a crib, but I would say that I strongly recommend the curtains.

Then you have a whole host of other things around the house. Do you need to clear cabinet space in your kitchen for the bottles? Do you need counter space for a bottle cleaner? You may not have to build as many things outside of the baby's room, but you're going to need to have the space ready for all that is coming that will take over your house.

I will say that I don't think you need a baby gate yet. I know that I've been a broken record about telling you that you need to make sure that you're ahead of the game, but a baby gate this early will only serve to trip you up or (heaven forbid) down the stairs. Your child won't walk until they're a year old (give or take) anyway, so you might as well wait until they get a little closer to that mark before you install the baby gates. You may want to map out where they are going and buy them and have them ready for when you see that first wobbly step, but you don't need to have them set up just yet.

You won't hardly believe it. When you're done getting everything ready, it will feel like the castle that was once your home is now a child's castle. Don't be sad. Isn't a bouncy castle, but it is great to feel that you have now prepared a fortress to protect and care for this child that you are about to have. What a great thing you just did for this kid.

The Second Trimester:

Okay, so your house is ready, but what else is happening during this time? So much. Check the apps that you hopefully got earlier, and you'll see your child has grown from a blueberry to a grapefruit. At least.

You should be continuing to have check-ins with your doctor every four weeks. These can be some of the revealing tests that you're coming up on, so it is okay to take a deep breath and understand the big things that are coming your way.

A lot of it will continue to look like what you've already seen. Blood pressure, weight, and baby's heartbeat will all be checked during every visit. There will be additional tests during this time too. Around 13-16 weeks, you'll have a chromosomal test. I don't know how it goes, but it can be a tough one to sit tight for and wait for the results.

Odds are, everything will be fine, but if there are chromosomal abnormalities, you may be referred to a specialist and you may need to have some really hard conversations with your partner. It's okay to feel sad and overwhelmed by these results. This book, unfortunately, cannot address the depth of what you may be going through, but there are plenty of resources to help you through this process.

My friends Dave and Val have four kids and their third child Lee has down syndrome. They found out during the chromosomal test that happened at the start of Val's second trimester. It was difficult news to process, but they both were very firm in their desire to have Lee and love him fiercely. Lee is such an important part of their family and they are so glad Lee is here to bring such joy to them all. As a close friend of mine, I've come to love Lee too and I can say with 100% certainty that if you have a Lee in your family, you'll be very lucky.

Around week 17-20 or so there will be another test to look at the baby's anatomy and the doctor can determine the biological sex of the child. This is usually when it is done, and it is up to you if you want to know the sex or not. There are also blood tests that your partner can take earlier that can show if there are y chromosomes present in her blood or not.

Females have xx chromosomes and males have xy chromosomes, so if there are y chromosomes found in her blood, it is a male and if not, it is a female. Not every doctor's office offers this test, however, and it can be expensive to do if insurance doesn't cover it. It is totally okay to wait an extra couple of weeks to find out. And it is okay if you and your partner decide you don't want to find out until the birth anyway!

Around week 24 or so there will be another test for glucose levels to determine gestational diabetes. This test usually takes a little bit longer, but you should get the results while you're at the doctor's office. Again, if needed, the doctor will refer you to a specialist who will help you determine the best course of action moving forward and how to continue to prepare for a healthy pregnancy.

Your partner is probably showing by now, and that can be very exciting. It can also mean a new wardrobe for her, which depending on your partner can be an exciting thing, a sad thing, and is always an expensive thing.

There is a good chance that they may also start something called "nesting." It is a very natural and normal biological thing that mammals do to prepare for their baby. Nesting may look different for each person in the couple, but for us, it always manifested in my wife buying a ton of clothes for our yet to be born baby. Luckily for my wallet, she went to a lot of second-hand stores.

I didn't mind the clothes that she picked out. If she had energy and excitement and passion for these clothes, I was more than happy to have her pick out all of the outfits for the baby. I certainly didn't care enough, and it brought her so much joy.

The part that I minded was the hour-plus long narrative that would accompany the return from the shopping trip when I would be treated to every thought she had when she was going through all of the clothes that she ended up buying and why she got them and what made this outfit just right for our kid and why it was special that she buys this specific onesie.

After our first child, I came to learn that we basically kept our kid just in a diaper for the first three months and rarely put on clothes. We were feeding and changing and napping so much that it didn't make sense for us to put on clothes, so we didn't. By the time our firstborn started wearing the hundreds of outfits that my wife had picked out for him, he barely fit into any of them.

The point wasn't the clothes. The point wasn't even the stories my wife told me about the clothes. The point was that my wife was preparing in her own way for the kid. She didn't have a porch to build or a crib to set up and she couldn't be near the paint while I painted the baby's room because the fumes aren't good for pregnant mothers.

Your partner is going to be preparing during this second trimester. The house that you see as your castle is their nest, too. Let them nest, and if they need your help to build something or move something, please do it.

All the Classes:

You may or may not have a sense for all of the classes you need to take. It's up to you but I would say that you may not need to take all of them. And if you and your partner work full time, it may really be feasible for you to take all of these classes while you're pregnant. I mean at this point, you really only have about six months or so left and there is just no way to take classes the whole time. Plus, you don't want to take all those classes! You need time to prepare the home, have a baby shower, visit friends, maybe take a baby-moon, and you do not want your calendar chock-full of classes.

That being said, you should absolutely take some classes.

I would certainly recommend a birth-class. Now your birth class will depend on what kind of birth you want to have. Is it important for your partner to have a natural birth without medicine (read: epidural)? You can still have that at the hospital and can often have a doula or midwife help you with that (more on doulas soon). If you are having an all-natural birth, you absolutely *need* to have classes for that. There is a LOT for you as the father to be aware of and to be prepared for in that case. Take that class.

Even if you are planning to have a birth with an epidural, without a doula, and just with what the hospital is offering, I would still recommend that you take a birth-class. It will help you and your partner feel prepared for what is coming next. The birth is obviously a biggie, and it is so impossible to predict. A class will help your partner be ready for what their body will go through and it will help you prepare for how to best be a good birthing partner when they are in labor.

You may also want to take a prenatal exercise class. This will help with the emotional and mental preparations for the birth process. This is obviously more for your partner than for you, but if you can be present, it will be helpful. You can also learn the exercises and practice them at home with your partner whenever they want. Again, depending on the kind of birth you are choosing to have, it may be essential that you help your partner prepare, as they may need another person for certain exercises.

There are also lactation classes that your partner may be wanting to take, but again this one isn't really for you. As much as I have advocated for you to be present for your partner, this may be one that you sit out. In fact, I don't know if they let men in on these classes.

Whether or not your partner does take lactation classes, it is important for you to be extremely supportive of the breastfeeding processes and decisions that happen. Breastfeeding is not easy (an understatement if ever there was one) and it just isn't for everyone. If it is something your partner really wants to do, love and encourage them as best as you can. If it is something that comes easily, great! If it doesn't come easily, support them every time they try. If you end up needing to go with formula, that's fine! If your partner doesn't want to breastfeed and you only do formula, that is fine too! Whatever your partner is wanting, I would absolutely let them dictate the feeding expectations for those first couple of months.

Depending on your learning style, you may also want to take a parenting class. There are books about swaddling, communication, and what to expect in the first year, but some people are better "doers" than "readers." If you think it would be helpful for you to take a parenting class, go for it. There are a lot of benefits to that kind of class.

My friends Daniel and Maggie were the first in their friend group to have kids. They had a lot of advice from their parents, but they weren't sure that it was totally up to date. They read a lot of books, but still didn't feel like it was the same kind of learning as actually swaddling a baby doll would offer them. They signed up for a parenting class and to this day they swear that it was the best decision that they made pre-birth. When their firstborn came along, they said they felt totally ready for all of the small things they knew they were going to need to do in the first few hours, days, and weeks, because they had already practiced doing them!

Lastly, I would recommend a postpartum prep class for you and your partner. It is something that I wish we had done before our firstborn and I recommend it to every pregnant couple I talk with.

Your partner is about to have a pretty traumatic event happen to their body. They are going to be experiencing a wild range of emotions and mental and spiritual responses to what they are going through. Postpartum depression is very real and very hard to get over. Especially when you feel you need to be a good parent, it can be hard to take the steps to get out of the depression that can cloud even the smallest things in life.

The class isn't going to prevent postpartum, but it can give you and your partner the tools to understand what is happening and hopefully the wisdom to help her cope with this massive and sudden change in her life. This can be really hard for a new mom and as a new dad, you need to balance both taking care of your new baby and the new mom who has just gone through so much for your family.

To Doula or not to Doula, that is the Question:

You may or may not have heard of a doula before. Doulas are women that are specially trained to be birth partners for you and especially for your pregnant partner. Doulas have experience with hospitals, doctors, pregnancy complications, natural births, birth plans, and basically everything that has to do with the pregnancy and birthing process.

Doulas, or midwives, come from the tradition of women helping women give birth. In basically every culture in the history of humanity for forever, it made a lot of sense that when a woman was giving birth, the other women in the community would help coach, advocate for, and guide her during the pregnancy and birthing process.

Today, we have gotten a long way away from some of the cultural traditions around birthing practices. In many ways, modern medicine has reduced so many of the dangers of childbirth, which is absolutely fantastic! Still, there is something special about having a woman that has gone through childbirth before being able to be present in the hospital with you while you're experiencing labor.

For what it is worth, I would absolutely recommend a doula. It was something my wife asked for when we found out we were pregnant the first time. I was skeptical. A doula sounded like some backward practice, and I was a firm believer in modern medicine and the advances of technology.

It took me all of five minutes of meeting the doula to come around. She was perfectly okay with whatever birth plan we wanted, whatever hospital we chose, and basically, whatever it was we were looking for.

So, if a doula just goes along with whatever you say, you might wonder why you need one at all? Fair enough.

As a first-time dad, there is so much that you don't know. As a male, there is so much you can literally never know. As someone who is about to become a father, your focus is so much on your partner and your birthing baby that in the moment, you can forget your classes, your training, your birth plan, and all that you have been preparing.

I'm not saying it will happen necessarily, but I am saying that having someone there who is a third party who can be a great advocate for you and your partner, for your birth plan, and for what is best and healthiest for everyone involved is a fantastic and burden lifting way to go through labor and delivery.

Our doula was fantastic. She was recommended to my wife by her friend Ally and we could not have been more grateful. She helped us immensely in the pre-birth phase by talking us through a lot of planning and asking us a lot of questions about what we wanted the labor and delivery process to look like. She had so many questions that I never would have thought to ask and I was so grateful for her.

When the time came and my wife went into labor, we gave our doula a call and she met us at the hospital. When things were taking a little while, the doctor started pushing us towards a C-section. That was not what we had discussed, but I was so nervous I wasn't sure if I could tell a doctor no. Our doula calmly but firmly reminded him that our plan was to continue towards a vaginal birth as long as it was possible and healthy to do so.

A little while later, my wife gave birth to our firstborn through our planned vaginal delivery and we were all so grateful for our doula advocating for us and helping us to stick to our plan. Everyone was safe, healthy, and exceedingly happy with how the whole process went. We asked her back for our next three children, and it was the easiest decision we ever made.

Most doulas are willing to at least meet with you first and talk through what services they offer and what you can expect with them, and I would very highly recommend at least reaching out to have the conversation.

Hospital Logistics:

If you are a military history buff, this is your moment. Your D-Day plan will need to be so detailed and so ready for all variables that *General Eisenhower* would put you in command. If you are not a military history buff, just know that you need to have a high level of planning for an unprecedented move that will keep people talking about it a hundred years later.

The wild thing about pregnancy is that the labor can happen essentially at any time. That may sound ridiculous, but any time after six months (24 weeks), a fetus is considered medically viable, meaning that even if the baby is not fully developed, it has a good chance of living outside of the womb. All of a sudden nine months of prep time has been cut down to six and 24 weeks doesn't sound like a ton of time to prepare for everything.

In all likelihood, that won't happen to you, but you'll need to have everything in place before the 24-week mark to make sure that you and your partner are ready just in case that scenario does end up playing out. (Also, if you really want to get technical, and let's face it, why not with this book, many hospitals will do everything they can to resuscitate a baby born at 22 weeks, or just a little over five months, so you really have to be ready soon!)

It may seem simple, but there is a lot to plan for, and you need to be ready. When things start happening, your partner is going to need to focus on their body and the baby and you will need to be the one who can do all the little things to quite literally get from point A to point B with everything you need for a successful labor experience. We are going to break it down for you here.

Chances are you are bound by your healthcare provider as to what hospital you may be going to or what doctor may be attending to your partner. That being said, don't just take the first thing on the list. You'll need to make sure that your partner trusts the doctor immensely. Sometimes it can be worth the extra five or ten-minute drive if it means getting to a doctor that she prefers.

There are other things to consider as well. Does the hospital have a lot of the amenities that you are looking for; Are you wanting a bathtub in the room for a water birth? Do they allow doulas to be present? (Follow-up questions a later chapter—what is a doula? And do you want one?) Does the hospital have requirements and protocols that you agree with?

This is particularly essential for pregnant people in the age of COVID-19. Whether you like it or not, Covid has undeniably changed the landscape of healthcare and many hospitals have different rules and regulations regarding what they do and do not allow based on Covid rates in their area. If you are reading this book in a time when Covid is no longer an issue, congratulations—I'm so glad we've gotten past it as a global society!

In all seriousness, you need to look into the hospital policies to make sure you agree with them and are comfortable with what they ask of their patients. Some places may limit the number of people you can have in the room with the laboring mother. Others may restrict the number of guests that can visit after the birth. You just need to make sure you are aware of what the hospital will be doing and be ready to make sure you are compliant with their policies and procedures.

Most hospitals will let you tour their facility ahead of time, which is great. You can literally practice where you'll park, the checking-in process, and getting to the wing of the hospital for labor and delivery. There is something reassuring about knowing exactly where to go when the time comes.

Our friends Josh and Laura were having their first baby in the age of Covid. It took them a long time to find a hospital that they were comfortable with and an even longer time to plan out a virtual tour of the space. It wasn't exactly the plan they had in place when the initially got pregnant, but they were grateful for the chance to visually see the process of going through the hospital and up to the wing where Laura would give birth. They knew what to expect and understood the layout of the room when they got there. They both were very effusive in their praise of the virtual tour and assured me that if I ever had another (which I won't) that a virtual tour would be just as good as an in-person tour.

How to Help:

For some people, this doesn't need to be said. For others, this will be shocking news. The best thing that you can do to be helpful is to take the initiative to do all of the things discussed in this chapter. If you and your partner are talking about classes, don't make her schedule everything or wait for her to do all the research. Except maybe for the lactation class—let your partner handle that one on her own, but if you're going to be present, it is a good expectation for you to be planning what is going to happen.

Again, I shouldn't have to say this, but if you are taking on the mantle of baby proofing and baby prepping, you should really take the lead on getting

Second Trimester Real-Life Scenario:

Ryan and Molly love having kids. Ryan and Molly had five kids before they were 35. Were they needing to be checked on mentally for such decisions? Perhaps. But I can only say that as someone who has four kids. How someone has four kids and then opts in for another is beyond me. Year after year, Ryan and Molly had their "annual child" and no sooner did one come along than they started to prepare for their next one.

For them, they found a certain rhythm and groove in the process. I mean, if it is what you are doing for the better part of a decade, it makes sense that the couple would find out what worked well for them. They found a good pace and a good understanding of what to expect, but that did not happen right away.

Ryan still regrets how he approached things with the first pregnancy. He once was a very laid-back man and just took life as it happened. He figured everything would just kind of work itself out and assumed that nine months of pregnancy would be plenty of time to get everything done that needed to be done.

When Molly went into labor just two weeks early, Ryan panicked. He didn't have hardly any of the stuff around the house ready. The crib wasn't built, the changing station was still yet to be ordered, and there was a pile of unread books about pregnancy and fatherhood.

As Ryan was driving Molly to the hospital, he was excited for the birth, but felt awful about not taking the time to get all of the things done that he needed to get done around the house. He felt like he had failed in his first task as a father, which was to prepare for the baby's arrival and give the new child a good home to come into.

When they got to the hospital, Molly was diagnosed with false labor and braxton hicks contractions. Those can happen, especially so close to the due date. Had Ryan finished reading his books, he might have learned that braxton hicks contractions are irregular, don't get any stronger, don't last any longer, and eventually fade away. (For the record, I'm not trying to shame Ryan here, he is a good friend of mine and he is okay with his story being shared!).

They got back home, and Ryan immediately went to work. The room was set up quickly, but he knew he didn't have time to read all or prepare all the things he had initially hoped to get through before the baby was born. He talked with Molly and together they decided what to prioritize over the next couple of weeks.

Molly has always been a clever and willful woman. To this day she refuses to acknowledge if she really had braxton hicks or if she knew that an early labor scare would motivate Ryan to get things done that she wanted him to do. (If you knew Molly, you would know she had real contractions, but really really really wants to play up this angle that she masterminded a whole plan into tricking Ryan into building the crib).

Second Trimester Summary:

By now you are in full pregnancy mode. You and your partner have got a lot of things figured out and you're doing your best to balance enjoying life without children while you still can and getting everything ready as you prepare for the baby's arrival. This phase is about being as ready as you can be before the birth. It will take work, but now is when you have the time to do it. You still have a few months to prepare, your partner isn't so uncomfortable that they can't (or won't) help, and you'll be grateful down the road that you took the time early on to get things ready.

You need to start baby proofing the house and it is okay to get started on a lot of it now. Not only do you want to have everything in place before the baby gets here, but you're going to want to not have to look like an idiot in front of your newborn by struggling to open your own silverware drawer.

Get the baby's room ready! Let your partner pick the paint color and make sure you leave a window open when you paint. The fumes, while really bad for a pregnant woman, aren't great for you either dad. Go ahead and get a few of the big things. Some people may be wanting to get you things for a baby shower, but the big stuff is on you. Go ahead and get what you need to start setting up the baby's room and knock that part out.

Continue to be present at the doctor's appointments and be very supportive and as patient as you can with all of the tests and results that you'll get in the second trimester.

Sign up for a class. At least one class. You may sign up for more than one, but you may not sign up for less than one. Pick one class that you and your partner can go to together and make sure you go. If you aren't going to other classes, that's okay, but you should probably have a plan in place for how you are going to tackle some of what was covered in the classes.

Have a conversation with a doula. If you are even remotely curious about a doula, go ahead and schedule a conversation. There are a lot of benefits to having a doula, but it is not for everyone. Decide with your partner what is best for you and what you are both looking for during the birth experience. Again, if you aren't going to have a doula, you'll probably need to have a more full plan in place for the birth experience and a lot more responsibility will fall on you to advocate during the labor and delivery.

Get the hospital you want and tour it. Know where you're going and what to expect when you get there. Have the route mapped out and don't be ashamed of putting the destination in a map app just to make sure you avoid traffic and get there as quick as you can when the day comes. You've got this general.

Second Trimester Checklist:

☐ House Proofing

   ☐ Outlet covers

   ☐ Latches for drawers and cabinets

   ☐ Anchoring furniture

- [ ] Securing wall fixtures
- [ ] Strapping TVs
- [ ] Other house proofing needs _____
- [ ] House Prepping
  - [ ] Baby's Room
    - [ ] Paint (If needed)
    - [ ] Crib
    - [ ] Changing Station
    - [ ] Blackout Curtain
  - [ ] Kitchen
    - [ ] Space on counter
    - [ ] Space in cabinets/pantry
- [ ] Doctors 'Visits
  - [ ] Chromosome test
  - [ ] Biological sex test
  - [ ] Gestational diabetes test
  - [ ] Test to see if you're paying attention test (seriously—ask one question to the doctor!)
- [ ] Classes
  - [ ] Birth Class
  - [ ] Prenatal Exercise
  - [ ] Lactation

- [ ] Parenting Class
- [ ] Postpartum Class
- [ ] Doula/Midwife
  - [ ] Interview/Conversation with a Doula/Midwife?
  - [ ] Hire a Doula or Midwife?
- [ ] Hospital
  - [ ] Choose the hospital
  - [ ] Plan your route
  - [ ] Know the layout and where to go
  - [ ] Tour/Virtual Tour

Chapter 5

THE BABY SHOWER

T he baby shower is a unique thing. It doesn't neatly fall into a pregnancy timeline, so I didn't put it in any of the other chapters. This chapter is a bit of a break, but not from checklists. In fact, this will be the largest checklist in the book.

As far as when to do this on your timeline, that really is up to you and your partner. I sandwiched it in between the second and third trimester because that is generally when it happens. You need it to be late enough for you to have had time to organize, plan, prepare, and choose what you're hoping to get at your shower. You also need it early enough to be able to set up and put in place all that you got from your shower. Typically, showers fall somewhere in month six or seven, so depending on when you have yours, it'll be somewhere in the late second trimester or early third trimester.

You may be tempted to let your partner handle a lot of this, and maybe she will want to head this up. After all, the baby shower is often something that is mostly for the soon-to-be-mom. It's okay if she takes the reins for a lot of the planning and a lot of what appears on the list, but just like how it is important for you to go to the doctor's offices, it will be important for you to be involved in the baby shower.

You are going to get a lot of things. The smallest person in your house will have the most stuff and it will be everywhere. It will be important for you to know what you're getting, why you're getting it, how to use it, and what is expected of you to get it.

If you're the planning type, you might go all out. Maybe you want to call your partner's friends and family, pick the date, and set up all the decorations, food, games, and everything. It is okay if your partner does a lot of that work. And it is okay if your friends and family want to come too.

Since this book is strictly about pregnancy preparation, I am not going to spend a lot of time on party planning. That is going to be a separate thing you'll have to handle on your own. Best of luck to you in all your event planning endeavors.

We will, however, be focusing on what you need, as far as baby supplies go. Once the party is set, you can register (just like a wedding registry) at places like Target, Bed Bath and Beyond, Baby List, Buy Buy Baby, Baby Baby Baby (kidding about this last one—I'm just saying there are a lot of options).

When we look at all you'll need, I'm not going to make decisions for you. I know, I know, it would be a lot easier if I could just tell you what to get and you would just do it. But it doesn't work like that. You and your partner have specific needs, a specific living space, and preferences for what you want when it comes to raising your child.

Instead of giving you all the answers, I'll do my best to lay out a lot of the options and will, from time to time, share why we got what we ended up getting and if we found it to be helpful or not.

Items

This is pretty close to exhaustive, but don't feel like you need everything on here. Hopefully, it helps to sort through what you need and what your options are, but feel free to make this list your own; add what you need, and leave off whatever doesn't work for you.

There will be a lot more on the checklist at the end of the chapter, but this will hopefully be a good sense for what to expect

☐ **Bedding and Furniture:** as mentioned before, you probably should already have a crib, a changing station, and a glider or rocker for the baby's room. Those are big things and you probably don't want to chance it on someone else getting it for you or not. Here are lot of the smaller things you can expect.

☐ Crib Sheet: you're going to want at least three. You don't want to do laundry all the time, and you want to make sure that when the baby pees on the sheet you have a couple of back-ups. Four isn't a bad idea.

☐ Waterproof Mattress Pads: again, at least two so that when there is pee on one, you can switch out with another. This way, even if there is pee on the bed, you don't have to forego the whole mattress in the middle of the night.

☐ Storage baskets: you know your organizational style better than anyone, but you're going to have more stuff than you can imagine, so you're going to want to find ways to manage that.

☐ Baby size hangers: one of the little things I never would have thought about. Maybe the hangers come with the clothes, but if they don't, you'll need them.

☐ White noise machine: this will help with sleep for sure. Get one.

☐ **Car Seat and Stroller:** you are going to want these soon so you can start getting them set up in the third trimester.

   ☐ Umbrella stroller: these are the quick folding ones. You won't use it probably until the baby is much older, but these are so nice and light-weight and they don't take up a lot of room. Doesn't hurt to get it now and be ready.

   ☐ Deluxe stroller: whatever your needs are in life, there is a stroller option for you. Running stroller? City stroller? Shaded stroller? They have them all. Find whatever is going to be your need and find a stroller to match. Make sure it is durable and ready to go for a lot of folding and unfolding over the next couple of years.

   ☐ Car seat: no matter what brand you go with, you'll find things to love and hate. A lot of options will have a car seat that also attaches to the stroller or a multi-year car seat that will expand as the baby grows. You do whatever is your priority, but make sure you find a good deal for your lifestyle.

   ☐ Seat Liner: this was one we didn't think about until the first time that it happened and then we never went without it again. It is simple. Basically, it is just a plastic lining over your car seat so that if/when a diaper eruption happens, you aren't also cleaning the whole seat. Worth it.

☐ Mirror: the little car mirror is another thing that is easy to miss or forget about, but you'll be grateful to have it set up so that if any parent is needing to go solo, they can still look back and see their beautiful baby's face.

☐ **Clothing:** the big thing you need to know about clothing is that none of the sizes make sense. I mean in theory they do, but the geniuses in the baby clothing industry have chosen to organize their sizes based on age. 0-3 months, 3-6 months, 6-9 months, 9-12 months, 1T, 2T, etc.

These sizes sound nice, but there are two things to know. First, no two brands have the same measurements. If you have something from Baby Store One that says 0-3m, you will have something else from Baby Store Two that will say 3-6m and will be the same size.

The second thing to know is that those sizes just don't coordinate to every single baby. I'll never understand why clothes aren't organized by weight like diapers are. A baby that is born 10lbs is such a different size than a baby born 6lbs, and there is no reason why they should both be in 0-3m. It's dumb, get used to it being dumb.

☐ Swaddling blankets: again, you'll need more than you think. We had eight, and I wish we had at least a dozen. They get dirty quickly and you don't want to wrap your baby in their own spit up. They need to be swaddled for every nap and every night, and those are a lot of swaddles in the early days.

☐ Cloth diapers: this is up to you and your partner. Depending on how often your kid goes to the bathroom, you'll see a big financial benefit, especially come the second year of use. There is more time in the laundry room and in prepping the diapers, but the savings can balance out the extra time. If you're worried about not wanting to be around poop and pee a ton, that's going to happen no matter what, and in about a week you won't even think about it. Diapers will be the least of your concerns and you won't care if they're cloth or not. That said, I'd get diaper liners if you end up going this route.

☐ The rest of the clothing stuff, I don't have that strong of an opinion on. If you want a lot of outfits, pajamas, socks, no-scratch mittens, go for it. Some babies love that stuff. Some hate it. Unfortunately, you won't know until it is too late.

☐ **Toys and Gifts:**

☐ Books: start with board books. You're going to need them to be sturdy. And then when the baby is a little bit older, you're going to want these amazing things that babies cannot destroy. Indestructible books that they can chew on without chewing up, grab at without tearing. I don't understand why these scientists have dedicated their energy to this technology instead of being rocket scientists or brain surgeons, but thank God they did.

☐ Sensory toys: there are plenty of toys that you're going to want to get your kid, but not all of them will make sense developmentally. Early on, they really just need some black and white cards with basic shapes and some sensory toys. There are some subscription boxes you can get if you want to help you stay up to date with all of the developmentally appropriate toys. Mostly, I'm just letting you know that early on they don't need a lot.

☐ Photo albums/Keepsake book: this starts as something that is more for you and your partner, but I'll tell you that when your kid gets older, they'll appreciate being able to look back and see the pictures and the keepsakes. It sounds cheesy, but you should go ahead and get these and keep up with them.

☐ **Feeding:** this section totally depends on what you and your partner are going to do. For the first few months it is exclusively breastmilk or formula, so you're going to have really different needs based on what route you end up going. There are a few notes still.

　☐ Bottles: I didn't believe it the first time I heard it, but there are different lids for different ages. Babies have to work their way up to larger holes and bigger flow, so at first, they have different nipples for the bottles until they work their way up. These are not one size fits all. I mention this mostly for your budgeting needs.

　☐ Bibs: we just took our kids 'clothes off. Seriously. Way easier than trying to get them into a bib. Go bib if you want, but odds are you're going to end up with stuff on the clothes, anyway. Bibs, I think, are for restaurants. If you're home eating, who cares if the baby is shirtless?

　☐ Pacifiers: you aren't supposed to start these right away! Who knew? I didn't! You do now! Apparently, you have to wait at least four-week or so before you try those suckers out. Another great dad joke, but the information is real!

☐ **Safety and Health:** this section has a lot to do with the baby's health, but even more to do with your peace of mind. One of the most terrifying things is thinking about your baby's safety and it can be easy to worry and worry and worry. Be prepared and feel better about things.

☐ Baby monitor: you get whatever kind you want, but what we found to be the most helpful was not the video screen and audio speakers. That was fine, but what really put our minds at ease was a device that you could attach as a sock that would monitor the baby's heart rate and oxygen levels and would send an alert to our phones if either fell below a certain level.

☐ I cannot stress enough just how helpful this was for us to be able to sleep (when we could sleep, that is). To trust that no matter what happened, we would get an alert if the baby needed to be woken up was a game changer for us.

☐ Before we got that set up for our firstborn, I spent the first night home from the hospital sleeping on the floor next to the bassinet at the base of our bed. I couldn't hardly shut my eyes before I would pop up and look inside the bassinet to make sure our firstborn was still breathing normally. The next night, we got the monitor sock attached and working properly, and I was able to finally get some rest.

☐ The alert only went off twice in the first year of our kid's life, and I was scared out of my wits when it went off, but I was so incredibly grateful to have that alert go off so that I could respond to my child's needs in the moment. **One of the biggest things I recommend to new parents is the sock monitor.**

☐ Baby laundry detergent: whether or not your baby is hypo-allergenic, it is a good idea to start washing your clothes in the baby-safe laundry detergent. That way when you all get home from the hospital; all of your sheets and clothes are already prepared and ready for your baby to smoosh their cute face all over everything you own.

☐ **Bathroom Needs:** a lot of this stuff you won't need until they are much older, but it is a good idea to have things ready so you aren't running out last minute to get things.

☐ Bath tub: it is a weird thing to get a little mini baby bathtub to put in your bathtub (or your sink if it is big enough) but that's something you have to do.

☐ Thermometer: babies are tougher than you think and more delicate than you think. The nice warm bath you want is probably not great for the baby. Go ahead and get the water thermometer so that you can make sure the water isn't too hot or too cold for the baby when they're ready for bath time.

☐ Diaper rash ointment: hopefully you won't ever need it, but if you do need it, you really do not want to run out to the store to go get it. You want it to be right there, right when you need it.

☐ Bath kneeler/stool: this is on you. Do you need it? Are you able to crouch down and sit next to the tub? Are you planning to get in the tub? You decide what is right for you and get what you need for your increasingly older and older knees and back.

Baby Shower Real-Life Scenario:

Sara and Alex were great planners, and that went for everything they were doing in their pregnancy. They also trusted each other a lot. Early in the second trimester, they began planning for their baby shower. They knew that there was going to be a lot on the list, so they decided to divide and conquer.

Sara took a lot of the feeding and clothing needs and was excited to get straight to work on researching and deciding how much of everything they would need.

Alex was tasked with bedroom supplies, car seats/strollers, and safety and health. The two decided that whenever there was a decision to be made that was "important enough," they would share with each other what they had found and why they wanted their partner to weigh in on it. After Sara started sharing "important" discussions on swaddling in green blankets vs. swaddling in blue blankets, Alex felt he needed to clarify what he felt the word "important" meant.

When Alex was researching, he found different car seats that plugged into strollers. Choosing one set of car seats almost made them choose the stroller to go along with it. While he figured that he would do most of the car seat installation, Alex wanted to make sure Sara was okay with the stroller that went along with it. Sara quickly let Alex know that she did not want that kind of stroller because one of her girlfriends found it to be difficult to get in and out of the car on her own.

Over the next month, the two went back and forth with their research and their recommendations to one another, and finally they were able to compile what they called their "Ultimate Baby Shower List." They shared the list and the registries (that's right, they registered at multiple places) with their friends and family and when the date came, they had an amazing baby shower.

They didn't get everything on the list that they had asked for, but because they had done such good research and had communicated so well on the list, they knew exactly what else they needed in order to have all that they wanted to have at the house ready for the baby's arrival. They were so prepared and when the baby came, the house was full and ready with everything they could have ever wanted in order to make sure they could meet every need that their newborn had in the first three months.

Baby Shower Summary

Whenever you choose to have your shower, there is a good reason to be involved in it. Don't just punt on this one and let your partner handle it all. If she is picking out the car seat, but you're the one expected to install it, your input matters in that car seat selection.

Take your time to go through the list below and see what makes sense for you. My guess is that you aren't going to want or need everything on this list. But you will probably see some things on here that you'll need to think through and talk through. There are a lot of things you need and a lot of things you don't need. Unfortunately, you won't know until the baby comes what all you wish you would have had more of and which thing you probably could have done without.

Still, it is better to be overly prepared and have options than to not have what you need at a critical moment when the baby needs something the most. A baby shower is a good way to prepare not just for all of the "stuff" but for all of the little things your baby will need in their daily life and how you can be a good provider for all of those needs.

Baby Shower Checklist—This is a biggie

- [ ] **Bedding and Furniture**
  - [ ] Crib
  - [ ] Crib Mattress (if not included with the crib)
  - [ ] Pack 'n 'Play
  - [ ] 2-3 Waterproof Mattress Pads
  - [ ] 2-3 Fitted Crib Sheets
  - [ ] 2-3 Sheet protectors
  - [ ] Bedding
  - [ ] Crib Toy/Mobile
  - [ ] Dresser
  - [ ] Changing Table
  - [ ] Changing Pad
  - [ ] 2-3 Changing Pad Covers
  - [ ] Bassinet
  - [ ] 2-3 Bassinet Sheets

- ☐ Glider or Rocker
- ☐ Storage Baskets
- ☐ Toy Chest
- ☐ Lamp
- ☐ White Noise Machine
- ☐ Baby Sized Hangers

☐ **Car Seat & Stroller**

- ☐ Umbrella Stroller
- ☐ Deluxe Stroller
- ☐ Car Seat (2 if you have 2 cars)
- ☐ Extra Car Seat Base
- ☐ Storage Console (as needed)
- ☐ Car Mirror
- ☐ Waterproof Seat Liners

☐ **Clothing**

- ☐ 4-6 Snap tees
- ☐ 4-6 Body Suits
- ☐ 1-2 Hats
- ☐ 1-2 No Scratch Mittens
- ☐ 9-12 Pairs of Socks (These will inevitably get separated and lost in your washer and dryer and

there is no book to help you not lose these/lose your sanity when you lose baby socks)

☐ 2-3 Pajamas

☐ 8-12 Swaddling Blankets

☐ 4-8 Pairs of Pants

☐ 4-8 Footies

☐ Coming Home Outfit

☐ Seasonal Clothing (Swimsuit? Jacket? Ugly Christmas Sweater?)

☐ Baby Sling (Clothing for you to wear the baby in)

☐ **Toys and Gifts**

☐ Books

☐ Activity Mat

☐ Sensory Toys

☐ Photo Album/Keepsake

☐ **Feeding**

☐ Breast Pump and Accessories

☐ Breast Milk Storage Containers

☐ Steam Sterilizer Bags

☐ Nursing Bras, Pads, Soothing Ointments, etc.

☐ Nursing Pillow

☐ Nursing Stool

- [ ] 8-12 bottles and nipples
- [ ] Bottle Warmer
- [ ] Bottle Sterilizer
- [ ] High Chair
- [ ] Splat Mat
- [ ] 3-5 Baby Spoons and Bowls
- [ ] 4 toddler Cups
- [ ] 10+ Burp Cloths
- [ ] 3-4 Bibs
- [ ] 4-6 Pacifiers
- [ ] 2-3 Teethers

- [ ] **Safety and Health**

  - [ ] Baby Monitor
  - [ ] Alert Sock
  - [ ] Safety Gates
  - [ ] Safety Locks and Straps
  - [ ] Humidifier
  - [ ] Thermometer
  - [ ] Nasal Aspirator
  - [ ] First Aid Kit and Baby Medicine
  - [ ] Nail Clippers or Scissors
  - [ ] Baby Toothbrush/Finger Brush

- ☐ Brush and Comb
- ☐ Baby Safe Cleaning Supplies
- ☐ Gentle Laundry Detergent
- ☐ Night Light

☐ **Bathroom Needs**

- ☐ Baby Bathtub
- ☐ Baby Shampoo
- ☐ Baby Washcloth
- ☐ Shampoo Rinse Cup
- ☐ Bath Toys
- ☐ Bath Kneeler/Stool
- ☐ 2-3 Towels
- ☐ 4-5 Washcloths
- ☐ Diapers
- ☐ Diaper Pail Refills
- ☐ Wipes
- ☐ Diaper Rash Ointment

Chapter 6

THE THIRD TRIMESTER

During the third trimester, the fetus continues to grow exponentially in weight and size. The lungs are maturing quickly and the fetus shifts to position itself head down. By the end of the third trimester, or just before birth, the fetus is usually between 19 to 21 inches long and weighs, on average, between 6 to 9 pounds.

This chapter is going to encourage you to focus on some harder conversations. They're hard, yes, but they're much easier to have now than they will be once the baby is born. And of course, we'll take a look at the third trimester.

Because you've done such a good job getting ready and preparing for the first two trimesters, you are going to be able to do a lot of these things that many couples don't actually get to.

Hard Decisions

Come Up With a Name:

Okay, just because it is fun doesn't mean it isn't hard! I know a lot of couples that have struggled with this one. Hopefully, you won't, but it is okay if you do. Maybe you have some initials you really like, or maybe you have some certain family names to work from, but there is no right or wrong way to go about this.

My only advice is that there is a special joy in loving your child's name. Maybe you might not be absolutely in love with the name the moment that your partner says it, but give it time and maybe it will grow on you. If you really cannot stand it, or if you have a great reason for not loving it, be honest about that.

If you have a tricky last name, make sure the first and middle names sound good together. And make sure that the initials don't spell out something embarrassing. You may be surprised at the thoughtlessness of parents when it comes to their kids 'initials.

If you get stuck, there is no shame in looking at baby name books or even listening to baby name podcasts. Yes, there are baby name podcasts. If you can think of a topic, I guarantee you there is a podcast on it.

At any rate, you're getting down to the last few months, and it is best not to wait until you're in the hospital to come up with a name. My friends Brad and Christine were both dug in around a specific name. Each person loved their idea and hated the other person's suggestion. Neither budged all the way until labor started. At that point, Brad suggested giving in and letting Christine's name choice be the first name and his name choice be the middle name. Both started calling the child their own preferred name, and in no time, they were both furious with each other.

A year later they got the name changed to one they both agreed on, but it took a lot of money and a lot of embarrassing conversations with their family and friends. I wish this were a made-up story.

Make a Will:

While you may not think you need a will, you now do. You may not have had enough assets in your life to think that a will would be needed. You now have something so important that you do not want to leave things to people's best guesses. This will take a little bit of time, but it isn't too terribly expensive, and it will give you peace of mind to know what would happen in the event of your death.

Along with this, and to be included in the will is whoever you decide will get custody of your child if you and your partner should both die. I know it sounds farfetched and sad and you may not want to think about it, but in the United States, if you do not specifically name someone in the will, anyone can come forward and a judge will decide.

Please name someone in your will.

Talk Through Parenting Decisions:

Hopefully, you and your partner are compatible enough and are on the same page about a lot of what you want the first few months to look like. Do not assume that you are on the same page about things. Odds are you were brought up very differently and there are certain things that you really want to take forward from your own upbringing and many things you are wanting to leave behind when it comes to raising your own child.

The biggies here that I would really recommend you having a serious conversation to talk through are sleep training and feeding. There are a lot of little questions about which toys you find appropriate, if you want to try and teach your child sign language to communicate a few basics about hunger, thirst, diaper changes, help, etcetera (you should totally do sign language) and what you want to do about screen time (you should wait until your kid is two) but those things are smaller in scope and in how they impact the whole family.

Feeding is fairly simple at first. Breastfeeding or formula are your only options for the first few months. Whether or not your partner is wanting to, or is able to breastfeed, the diet itself is pretty much set for the kid. But what do you do afterward? Is your partner adamant about breastfeeding until year two or three? The World Health Organization recommends up to the age of four. It isn't the most ridiculous thing for a mom to want to continue to breastfeed.

How does that impact the child? Are they able to transition to solid foods? Do you do baby-led-weaning? Do you ask them to try everything you make for them or just let them eat whatever they choose? There are pros and cons to whatever you end up choosing, and I'm really not here to tell you what you should or shouldn't do. I'm just saying that you need to talk through this with your partner.

Similarly, what you want to do for sleep training isn't a huge question at first. The earliest you would do sleep training is at three months anyway, and it's probably more likely that you wouldn't start until five or six months. Still, it is good to know now so that you can plan and prepare.

There are plenty of books out there with a lot of great methods and suggestions. Many of your friends will tell you what did or didn't work for them. Again, it is less about what you choose and more important that you are on the same page as your partner.

My friends Mark and Laureen assumed they were in agreement, but when Mark wanted to let their firstborn cry it out, Laureen was horrified. She had assumed they would do a no-cry sleep method. They both thought the other person was so wrong for thinking what they thought and their constant fights around how to handle it when the baby wouldn't sleep compounded the difficulties of the sleepless nights.

Eventually, their pediatrician recommended a method that worked well enough for both of them, and in two weeks, their child was sleeping through the night. Still, it was hard for them for several months and without that timely suggestion, they might have continued fighting until the kid was old enough to figure out sleeping on his own.

You will inevitably disagree with your partner on things. It is going to happen. It is normal. You can do your best to talk through as much as possible and I am 100% certain that you will have a disagreement with your partner about how you raise your child.

It's really hard, and that is okay to admit. No matter how good you may have been at working through your disagreements before, there is a new underlying current that appears when you aren't on the same page about a parenting decision. When you disagree with your partner, there is a part of you saying, "I think your suggestion isn't what is best for our child," and even if that is just implied instead of explicitly said, it brings a new dimension to your hard conversations when you're trying to find agreement and common ground.

The hope here is that you will find ways to minimize the disagreement and time spent arguing over things. The more that you understand how to communicate through these disagreements, the better for you and for your child.

Have a Plan for the Worst-Case Scenario:

You don't want to do this, but you have to do this. You need to talk through what may happen if the labor and delivery do not go well. If it is a conversation that is really hard to bring up, just frame it like this: "You know how if you bring an umbrella it doesn't rain, but if you forget your umbrella at home, it pours?" and then your partner will think you're an idiot for comparing labor and delivery to forgetting an umbrella and chances are they'll laugh at you and hopefully be in a good enough mood to talk through this.

Seriously though, it is important to talk through together what you want to happen in case things aren't going well. Do you want to prioritize the baby's life or the mothers? What do you want to do in the event of a stillbirth? How do you want the doctors to handle things? Do you want a chaplain to be available or is that the last person you want to talk with?

This will be a part of your fuller labor and delivery plan, but I think it usually goes best as a separate conversation. You want the labor and delivery plan to be a more enjoyable talk than this.

Detail Your Birth Plan:

If ever there were a section where you absolutely need your partner's input, this is it. Do not go this way alone. I don't care how many books you've read or how knowledgeable you think you are about what the best practices are for childbirth, this is your chance to really listen to what your partner wants and not push back too hard unless there are some very serious disagreements in what the plan is. If you've decided earlier to have a doula, this can be something you talk through with your doula as well to help you.

There are a lot of pieces to include in the labor and delivery plan. The first part is assuming a normal and smooth process. Basically, a best-case scenario. If everything went perfectly, what would you do?

What ambience do you want in the room? This is real—what music and lighting do you want? Are there aromas your partner wants or absolutely does not want to smell during labor and delivery?

What position do you want to be in? This can range from a standard bed to a bathtub to a shower to standing to whatever position you and your partner (and your doula) have talked through.

What kind of pain management are you okay with? Natural (non-medicated) births have become increasingly popular lately, but it is a hard plan to stick to when the partner is constantly being offered an epidural by the staff. How do you want to handle it?

Do you want assisted delivery options? Hospitals can do forceps (I was a forceps baby!), or vacuum suction deliveries.

After the birth, what do you want to happen? Are you the one to cut the umbilical cord? Do you want the baby on the mother's chest right away? Are you wanting to do skin to skin bonding as well? (You do, but the question is when?) Are other people allowed in the room? Do you want the baby to sleep with you or to be taken care of by the hospital staff for the first night? This may depend on the hospital and might need to be considered in your hospital selection process.

What are the variables you will and will not allow for? Is a C-section the absolute last resort for you, or are you okay with it as soon as the doctor suggests it? As I shared earlier, we did not want a C-section, and it was very helpful for our doula to advocate for that part of our birth plan.

It is probably helpful to be a little flexible with the plan when you share it with the medical staff that you'll be working with. Maybe think about phrasing things like, "We really prefer to have option A over option B," or, "Unless it is absolutely medically necessary, we would like to avoid option X at all costs."

The birth plan isn't meant to be a hard and fast binding contract type of agreement. It is meant to be the guide as you all are going through the labor and delivery. It is best to think through it all beforehand when you are a little more level-headed and a little out of the intensity of the moment so that when the actual labor and delivery start, you are ready to handle what happens.

The Third Trimester:

So far, you've been coming to the doctor every four weeks or so. That is going to escalate during this last trimester. You'll probably be scheduled for visits every two weeks until week 36 and then once a week until delivery. You're in the home stretch now and every visit is going to be an important one.

You'll probably share the birth plan with your medical staff as soon as you get it done. Hopefully that is no later than week 30 or so, but it really wouldn't hurt to get that done earlier. The more time that the medical staff has to understand your plan, the better.

Depending on the hospital, you'll probably also be offered the Tdap (tetanus, diphtheria and pertussis) vaccine during one of the early visits of the second trimester. If you travel internationally a lot, there is a chance you may have an up-to-date Tdap but generally speaking, you probably don't and it is a really good idea to be up to date on your immunizations before the baby comes.

In week 35-37, there will be a pelvic exam for your partner. It is a kind of progress report on how her body is adapting to the changes and how ready it is for the labor and delivery phase. I'm not going to lie, you shouldn't call it a progress report in front of her. There will also be a test for group B streptococcus at this point, which is just a test for a certain type of bacterial infection that can be really bad for the baby right after birth. It's just a test, and if there are complications, the hospital will direct you on what the next steps are for you.

After 37 weeks, you're checking in weekly to really get all of the constant updates and to make sure the baby isn't in breach. Breach just means the baby is in a position where they are going to come out butt-first, and while it isn't impossible to deliver that way, it is almost a guaranteed C-section these days. You want your child to come out head-first, especially if you're wanting a vaginal delivery.

At this point, your partner is probably very large and very uncomfortable. Do everything you can to help. Sleep on the couch if she needs the whole bed. Bring ice if she is hot and tea if she is cold. Run yourself ragged getting her every little thing. Unless she is tired of you doing everything for her and wants her independence. Odds are that a lot of what you may do will be annoying to her.

Let's face it, she can only sleep in a couple of positions, her body is swollen in lots of weird places, she is carrying around an immense amount of extra weight, none of her old clothes fit, and as much as she loves being pregnant, she is ready for this baby to come out. It's understandable for her to feel the way she feels. Just do your best to be supportive when you can be, and out of the way when that is the most helpful thing for you to do.

Hospital Bag—Your Time to Shine:

I wanted to give the hospital bag its own section because it really feels very important for the dads to get the bag ready. You need to think about and coordinate what three people are going to need. That's right, this is your first time packing a back for your kid. It's also the last time for a while that you can get away with not packing diapers (the hospital has a lot) so enjoy that while you can.

For your partner, you're going to want to pack a robe or comfortable pajamas or whatever she wants to wear after the delivery. Pretty soon after you get there, she'll put on the hospital gown and after all that she goes through, she's going to be very sore and uncomfortable and it will be nice to have a nice cozy outfit for her.

You'll want to pack all the toiletries as though it were a long weekend. Toothbrush, toothpaste, shampoo, conditioner, and anything else your partner would bring on a trip. It may sound like a lot, but you just have no idea how long you'll be there, and if you end up sitting in the hospital for a while, it will be important to have a toothbrush. If she is breastfeeding, you'll want to pack nipple cream as well.

Pack pillows and blankets for her and for you. My friends Hannah and Chad went to the hospital for their 39-week appointment and Hannah's blood pressure was high, which led the doctor to decide to induce the pregnancy. Chad was proud of himself for bringing the hospital bag to the appointment "just in case."

After they got settled in the room and Chad mentioned several times how smart he was for remembering to pack the bag and bring it, Hannah sent him home to get her some pillows because she was so uncomfortable in the bed. He went ahead and got himself a pillow and a blanket as well, which was good because Hannah ended up spending three days laboring before delivering their firstborn.

Bring a copy of your birth plan. Even if you shared it with the hospital staff before, there is a good chance that a nurse or even a doctor may come in to attend to you who you may not have ever met before. Especially if you end up staying a while like Hannah and Chad did, you'll be grateful for the extra copies to be able to share with folks as needed.

Don't forget your other official documents like ID and insurance card. Maybe you keep those in your wallet normally, which is fine, but if you end up rushing out of the door in a hurry, then you really need to make sure you have your wallet. It isn't a bad idea to put a copy of the insurance in your bag or if you're a real digital native, go ahead and take a picture of it and have it saved to your phone just in case.

You're also going to want to pack a little bit like you're going on a long road trip. Bring your phone charger, things for relaxing (books and movies), and a ton of drinks and snacks. Let your partner pick out a lot of the snacks they want and then don't tell them when you go to the store and put them in the bag.

When I packed our first hospital bag, I was devastated when we got to the room and I opened it to find the chips were half gone. My wife looked at me sheepishly and said, "I knew they were there and I got hungry!" If your partner wants chips in your bag, buy an extra bag or two for your cupboards.

If you had stuff in your birth plan about ambiance, be sure you're bringing what needs to be brought from home. A lamp? A speaker? Soothing scents? Whatever you decided on in the birth plan, make sure it is in the bag.

Make sure your partner has everything they need for post-partum too. Whatever they may need for breastfeeding is going to start immediately. Bottles, nipple cream, pumps, pads, nursing bras, all of it comes in handy on day one. So, whatever your partner wants, as far as that goes, it should all be in there.

A lot of the baby stuff will be provided by the hospital. You don't need to bring the whole baby bathtub you just got, for instance. The diapers and wipes will be at the hospital too along with plenty of swaddling cloths. An outfit for coming home in is nice though, and whatever else your partner wants to make sure you have for your little one.

Other than that, be sure to have whatever reference books you may want, like this book, obviously!

Does this feel like too much for one bag? Okay, I'll be honest, after our first child, we did one bag of the essentials. I carried pillows and blankets separately, and we had an entirely separate (somewhat smaller) bag full of snacks.

Third Semester Real-Life Scenario:

Joe and Emily were pregnancy pros. They had three kids and were about to have their fourth. (Before you ask, no, Joe and Emily are not code names for me and my wife!).

They had experienced natural birth, a C-section, multiple hospitals, and felt that they had a handle on all that pregnancy had to offer. That was until they got into a car accident when Emily was 34 weeks pregnant and she had to be rushed to the hospital.

It was very scary for everyone involved, and things were touch and go for both Emily and the baby for a while. Joe, who wasn't hurt in the accident, was so nervous and anxious. He had arranged for his mom to stay with their three kids so he could be at the hospital with Emily, but other than that, he felt helpless.

All of their hard work on birth classes and plans seemed out the window while Emily was in surgery. He didn't even have the hospital bag he had spent so much time on.

After some pretty anxious hours passed in the hospital waiting room, Joe finally got the news that Emily and the baby were okay. They both needed to stay at the hospital for a while so that they could get strong enough to come home, but both were going to be just fine.

When they were talking about the experience later, Joe shared about all of the anxiety he had while Emily was in surgery. Emily smiled and patted Joe's face lovingly. "Imagine what you would have felt if we had been unprepared!" she said.

"What do you mean? We were unprepared for that car accident!" Joe replied.

"Yes, but we had our wills made up, a plan in place that the doctor knew about regarding our medical preferences in whose life to save, and what to do if the worst things happened."

Joe thought a minute, and then thought about how right Emily was. Joe was the kind of person who could easily let his mind go down a rabbit hole of "what-ifs" and knowing that they had dealt with some of the most difficult "what-if" scenarios together probably made things easier for him than he realized at the time.

Thankfully, none of those things happened, and Joe and Emily were able to happily head home with their new baby a couple of weeks after the accident.

Third Trimester Summary:

You're doing great so far and you're almost there. The finish line is in sight and you want it almost as bad as your partner does. Almost. Okay, probably not. She really really wants to be done with being pregnant by now.

Now is the time to have some hard conversations before the baby comes. They aren't all fun talks to have, but you need to make sure you have them. Whether you're picking out a name or picking out custody for when you come up with your will, make sure you and your partner are talking through everything and find what is right for your family.

Talk through some parenting decisions if you haven't already. It's better to find out now that you don't see eye-to-eye on things than it will be to find out at 2am while holding a crying baby.

Make a birth plan that includes the worst-case scenarios. Hopefully, you won't ever need to use it, but it is much better to have it and not need it than to need it and not have it.

Keep doing what you've already done well and make sure you keep showing up to the doctor's visits. Especially this late in the game, you never know when you may pop in for a regular check-in only to be told that they are going to induce you or that the labor is about to start. Things can really happen at any moment. And while that is maybe a little terrifying, you've also done a great job preparing for this and you are totally ready to be a dad!

Third Trimester Checklist:

- ☐ Pick out a name
- ☐ Make a will
- ☐ Plan for the worst-case scenario
- ☐ Develop a Birth Plan
- ☐ Talk through parenting preferences
- ☐ Doctor's Visits
  - ☐ Tdap vaccine
  - ☐ Share birth plan with medical staff
  - ☐ Pelvic exam
  - ☐ Group B streptococcus test
  - ☐ Baby in head-down position
- ☐ Pack the hospital bag(s)
  - ☐ Clothing for mom
  - ☐ Feeding/Nursing supplies
    - ☐ Bottles
    - ☐ Nipple Cream
    - ☐ Bras
    - ☐ Pads
  - ☐ Pillows/Blankets
  - ☐ Toiletries

- ☐ Toothbrush/Toothpaste
- ☐ Shampoo/Conditioner
- ☐ Phone
- ☐ Charger
- ☐ Books
- ☐ Movies/Entertainment
- ☐ Ambience (If needed)
  - ☐ Speaker
  - ☐ Lamp
  - ☐ Scents
- ☐ Going Home Outfit
- ☐ Snacks
- ☐ Drinks
- ☐ More Snacks
- ☐ All the Snacks

Chapter 7
THE BIG DAY

I t will happen. At any moment. You cannot predict it, though you can try and help it along with long walks or spicy food or even sex. None of those things will immediately make things start though. And you still won't know when it is going to happen. All you can do is to be ready for it when it does.

Firstly, I'll say that it doesn't (usually) happen like sitcoms. It isn't as though your partner will walk into the kitchen and say, "I think this is it," and then her water breaks and you're rushed off to the hospital and a scene change (and no sweat) later, you're holding a perfectly clean and healthy baby.

What is most likely going to happen is that your partner will start having contractions. If she wants, you can help her time them and ask her to measure intensity. This will help determine a couple of things. The first thing is that it will rule out braxton hicks. The second thing is that even if she is having contractions, it may be too early to go to the hospital. You can still go, both for braxton hicks and for early contractions, but a lot of the time, they'll just send you back home.

Once she has crossed the threshold, you should head to the hospital. The threshold is this very handy-to-remember "411 Rule": Contractions every four (4) minutes lasting one (1) minute for at least one (1) hour. When you hit that mark, pull up your traffic app, call the doula if you've got one, grab the bag(s) and make your way to the hospital.

Now, before you get into the labor room, they are going to pull your partner aside and make you wait for a bit. They are going to ask them if you are abusive and if they want you in the labor room. I'm not joking.

It is a good practice, and it makes a lot of sense, but when you are in the thrilling moment of getting to the hospital for labor, the last thing you want is to be pulled away from your partner and left in the waiting room while they give her an exam and make sure you're safe to be in the delivery room with her. It is okay. Breathe. You'll be with her soon enough.

Labor:

If you're concerned with technical definitions, labor is all of the time spent while your partner is dilating and pushing out the baby and the placenta. The delivery is just the pushing out of the baby (and technically the pushing of the placenta counts as a second delivery).

Labor can last a few hours or a few days. There is really no telling what to expect. And (not to get ahead of ourselves, but) whatever happens this first time for you may not be what happens on subsequent times either, so don't think you're getting a preview of future labors either.

The hospital staff will be in to talk you through what is happening and what the next steps are. Sometimes the steps come fast and sometimes they make take hours or even days. No matter what they say, you're ready because you've done the good prep work described to you in this book!

How to be Helpful:

This is absolutely the time to put your partner first. Whatever they need from you to make them feel better is what you need to be ready to give them. This is what the bags are for. If they need pillows or books or movies or songs or anything at all you need to give it to them.

There may be restrictions on what your partner is allowed to eat at this point, so be careful with how many of the snacks you end up eating. Make sure there will be plenty for her left when she's ready.

All the things you've brought from home are for her to use as she sees fit. Make sure the ambiance is right. Make sure you are doing all of the stretches and steps from the classes you've attended. Or make sure you're following your doula's advice.

Honestly, there isn't a ton of advice to give at this point. If you've done all the good work over the past nine months, you should be totally ready for this time. Just generally make sure you are doing all of the things that you have worked so hard to prepare for so that you can be fully present in this moment.

Delivery:

Once your partner is dilated enough to start pushing, the delivery has started. With my first child, my wife almost went too fast. The attending nurse barely had time to call the doctor in and told my wife to hold off on pushing until the doctor got there! It was very different our second time around when my wife had to push and push for hours.

Again, this is the time to listen to your partner, the medical staff, and possibly your doula. I have friends who basically just sat on the couch and offered their most encouraging words while their partner pushed. I alternated a lot between holding hands, singing a special song to my wife, and holding her right leg up while she pushed.

She will push and (assuming all goes well) your child will squeeze through the birth canal and enter into this world with a little cry and a lot of love.

Speaking of crying, it is okay to cry, dad. This is the most amazing thing you've witnessed, and it is okay to be overwhelmed with emotion when you see your child come into this world.

Immediately Afterward:

There is a second delivery that is the placenta. Sometimes it slides out fairly close to when the baby comes, but sometimes it can take a lot of extra pushing. As much as you want to care for the baby, you are going to have a little bit of time while the staff cleans up the child so you can help your partner finish strong.

It is going to be bloodier than you think it will be. If you are squeamish about blood, you most certainly do not want to watch the placenta being delivered. Once the placenta is passed, the staff will clean up your partner and you'll focus more on the baby.

Chances are you're going to cut the cord. It is meatier than you're going to be comfortable with. Even after four kids, I never got used to it. But the hospital staff will clamp it where you're supposed to cut it and you'll be just fine. There is basically no way to really mess this up.

They'll clean up the baby really quickly, do some measurements, and then they are going to want the baby to have skin to skin contact with the mom. It is really important for bonding and for the first hour (sometimes referred to as the golden hour) the baby will basically just sit on mom's chest. Maybe she'll be nursing, or maybe she'll just be laying there.

You'll maybe want to take some pictures, call your parents, or maybe you just want to leave the phone in the bag and take in the moment. It is a pretty incredible moment to be a part of and it is okay to just stand there and take it in.

The hospital staff will let you take some time to be in this room for a little bit, but soon they'll make you move rooms. Some of that depends on the hospital policies and some of it depends on how your partner is doing. After our second child, my wife still had some high blood pressure, so they had her on magnesium, and we couldn't really leave the room while she was on the medication.

They may get you some diapers and wipes and you should be ready to handle all of that kind of stuff while your partner rests. In fact, after that golden hour, don't be surprised if your partner really wants to sleep. Depending on how long you've been awake, you may want to sleep too, but unless it is an overnight time and the hospital has plans for taking care of your baby overnight, chances are, this is one of your first times to shine as a dad.

First off, I'll say that skin to skin is also important for your bonding with your baby. Don't be afraid to whip that shirt off and feel your newborn's body against yours. It will impact you. I still feel the spot on my chest where my baby first lay and when the nurse pulled her away to give to my wife, I could feel the outline of where she was on my body.

If your wife is sleeping, take time to familiarize yourself with what your needs are. Have the staff show you where the swaddling towels are, and feel free to take some practice swaddles. Your baby will escape. It will be frustrating. You will try again. They will escape again. Even if you practiced a lot at home or in classes, this baby knows things about escape that would make Harry Houdini's head spin.

You'll probably have to stay at the hospital for at least an extra day or two. Sometimes three. It depends on how labor and delivery went, but the staff should do a good job of telling you what to expect.

The baby will predominantly eat, sleep, excrete, and repeat. You can help swaddle them when they need swaddled and feeding them formula if that is the route you're going, and changing them when they need changing. If your partner wants to do it, obviously they should do it. But it is okay for them to really rest and let you handle most of what the baby's needs are.

One of the needs will be to clean the absolute gnarliest diaper change that child will ever have. Because the baby has been taking nutrients through the umbilical cord for so long, they have a lot of stuff inside them that needs to come out. It will come out as this unholy dark sticky mess that you didn't know could ever come from a human. It is called meconium if you want to impress people, but I don't care what you call it, it is unsettling. And it is all yours to clean.

Once the baby gets into the breastmilk and/or the formula, whatever they pass will be much more water soluble and easier to clean. I'm not saying it will be pleasant exactly, but it will be much better than that first demon poop.

When you're ready to go, you'll be glad that you already had the car seat installed and brought the "take home" outfit with you to the hospital. You may not exactly be sitting back and relaxing, but it is okay to feel good about what you've done to make sure you and your family are prepared for this moment.

Hospital Stay Real-Life Scenario:

Chris and Stacey were absolutely exhausted after three days of labor and delivery. Stacey maybe was a little bit more exhausted than Chris though, and he knew he needed to step up while she rested and tried to recover her energy.

The only thing was, Chris wasn't very prepared. The hospital staff seemed really busy and wasn't very good at telling him what he needed to do either. The nurse who was in charge told him that he could swaddle the baby and get it to sleep on its own in the little stand they had set up in the room, but she didn't show him how to actually swaddle the baby.

He had the cloth, but no knowledge. Stacey was already asleep, and he didn't want to wake her up just to do something as basic as swaddling. Chris was upset with himself for not taking more time to be better prepared for this moment. Still, he got out his phone and looked up videos on YouTube to begin his practice at swaddling his firstborn.

About half a dozen tries in, Chris was able to get a good, tight, but no too tight swaddle on his baby. He also was incredibly grateful for the fact that babies do not remember the first couple of years of life because he really messed up the first few tries.

Although he didn't know what to do at first, he was proud of himself for figuring things out on his own and being able to do some good for his child and for his partner. Chris felt emboldened by this experience, and from then on out, he was more straightforward with their needs when addressing the hospital staff.

This ended up being very good because Stacey's water broke more than 24 hours before delivery, which meant that she had a higher chance of infection and the hospital wanted to keep her longer to observe her. After one night in the small and cramped room, they were told they'd need to stay for at least two more days. Stacey was visibly upset, and Chris could tell that all she wanted to do was to head home to be with their new baby.

Chris wanted her health to be prioritized, and knew he probably couldn't get them released earlier, but he did talk with the hospital staff about getting them into a larger, more comfortable room. After some good advocating, the family was moved to the "deluxe room" at the end of the hall that was bigger than Chris 'apartment right out of college!

Stacey was grateful for Chris making the best of a hard situation, and the family felt much more comfortable for the duration of their stay at the hospital after the shift to the better room. Chris had plenty of time to show Stacey what he learned when it came to swaddling, changed his first of many more diapers yet to come, and went out a couple of times while Stacey and the baby were sleeping to pick up and bring back some of Stacey's favorite food.

Chris already had a small sample of how it would be impossible to plan for everything in fatherhood, but was proud of himself for how he responded to the unknown difficulties to be able to make life a little bit better for his partner and their child.

After they had spent a whole week in the hospital from labor to release, Chris and Stacey were grateful to head out and spend time in their home as a new family!

The Big Day Summary:

This is one of the shortest chapters in the book. This was done intentionally because when you are going through the labor, delivery, and the first few days with your baby, the last thing you want is to be looking through a book for what to do.

Honestly, this is why you've read this book and why you've made all of the plans that you've made. You have been working really hard for nine months to get everything ready so that when the big moment finally arrives, you can be fully present with the peace of mind knowing that you've done the best you can and prepared for everything you could have prepared for.

Right now, you don't need a huge outline or a summary of what you will go through during the labor, delivery, and hospital stay. Right now, you need the confidence to know that this will be good as a result of all the hard conversations, good work, and preparations that you've undergone.

So, if you're reading this at the hospital, put the book down and hold your partner's hand, or get her the snacks you packed, or swaddle that baby like you know how to do now, and quit worrying about preparing for the moment so that you can just be in the moment! Enjoy it, dad!

The Big Day Checklist

- ☐ Become a dad
- ☐ Live in the moment
- ☐ Advocate for my family
- ☐ Be the best dad

Chapter 8

YOUR BABY'S FIRST MONTHS

You've gotten through pregnancy, and that was the goal of this book, right? Why is there this additional chapter here about coming home? Well, I didn't want to totally leave you hanging. I mean, there are other books out there for what you should expect and what to be ready for in the first couple of weeks, but you really shouldn't have to buy a whole other book just for that. I've got you.

Or, I should say that you really do need to buy those other books, but I'll take you through the basics of what you can expect when you get home from the hospital.

Hopefully, you already have all that you need and know exactly where everything is. Maybe you have things set out next to where you'll need them (a baby bathtub in your bathroom, for example) or maybe you have a separate closet with all your baby stuff.

If you fall into the latter camp, go ahead and start putting things out where you're going to be using them. I'd start with the diapers at the changing station and the swaddles as well. We kept swaddles everywhere. Downstairs, upstairs, our bedroom, the baby's room. That was just us, though. I think most normal people probably keep them next to the baby's bed.

The baby's bed, by the way, should be in a bassinet at the foot of your bed. It is good for the first few months for you all to share a room. It's better for the baby's health, you can respond faster if they need anything, and it is easier for you when you're getting up and down throughout the night.

After the diapers and swaddles, you would make sure you know where that alert sock is. Practice putting it on for naps because it can be a pain in the butt to get it just right and when the baby is ready for some overnight sleep, the last thing you want is to be constantly adjusting that damn sock.

Once you have those basics down, I'd suggest heading to the kitchen to get whatever your bottle system is put together. You'll figure out pretty soon how often you need to wash and sterilize bottles, what your plan is for formula, how much you're going to need, what your partner's breastfeeding supplies are, and how much space all of that is going to take up on your counter and/or in your cupboards. You'll be surprised.

After the kitchen is set up, take some time to familiarize yourself with where all the little things are. The small hangers, the ointments, the bathtub, and all the great things you've spent time getting and organizing. Don't worry if you end up moving it all around a few times. Eventually, you'll find out where everything goes.

First Doctor's Visit:

When you come home, you'll soon be heading back out again to your first doctor's visit. In all likelihood, they made you set up the first visit before they let you leave the hospital. if not, set it up right away. You should have that visit within the first couple of days of leaving the hospital.

It is a great visit to have. Your pediatrician is going to love seeing such a cute baby and they will be wonderfully reassuring about how great your kid is. They will also put to rest all of the small worries you've accrued in the 24-48 hours of leaving the hospital and you'll feel so much better after having gone.

A big thing that happens to a lot of people is the concern over the lack of bowel movements. You'll be shocked when your doctor says it isn't a problem, even if it takes a few weeks. You'll double check and make sure you heard her say "weeks" and not "days" but she'll be right and you'll feel better, even if you feel a bit dubious. In no time, your little one will be pooping, regularly and you'll wish you never worried about it.

You'll also be reassured to learn that babies go cross-eyed all the time! I was so concerned when we brought our firstborn home that their eyes were constantly crossed. I had no idea that this was going to happen, and I was worried that at some point, they might stay that way. The early doctor's visit helped me to learn that there was nothing to be concerned about and that this is something that plenty of babies do all the time.

When you are done with the first visit, you'll get scheduled for your next visit. That is going to be the routine for a while. Over the next 18-24 months, you are going to have check-ups and check-ins, vaccines, and updates every few months. For our firstborn, we loved having such constant contact with the doctor to be able to ask all the questions that built up between visits.

We kept a list going on a notepad in the kitchen (because we are elder millennials who didn't use a note app or anything on our phones) and would take the list to the doctor every time we went. Every single time, the doctor was great and she helped answer all of our questions.

Don't be afraid to ask anything you want. This is their job and believe it or not, they usually really enjoy having parents be so involved and curious about their child's health.

It is much better than being an uninvolved or apathetic parent, and the doctor will be happy to see you take such an interest in your child.

Your Baby's First Months Summary:

Take a deep breath and take time to set up all of the great stuff you've gotten over the past several months. Hopefully, you'll have most everything you need and you won't need to have too many emergency runs to the store to get something completely unexpected. If you've followed the book so far, I'd say you should be fairly well prepared for coming home.

In addition to all of the logistics, take care of yourself when you get home. They tell you to sleep when the baby sleeps, and honestly, that can be kind of hard for the dad. The mom is usually sleeping when the baby sleeps, but you may feel the need to get the rest of the things around the house set up.

It's okay for you to sleep, too. It's okay for you to rest. And while you want to be there for your partner and for your new baby, you also need to be there for yourself and your needs.

You've prepared well, you have everything you need, you did a great job getting through pregnancy, and now you're ready to be a great dad!

Your Baby's First Months Checklist:

☐ Get the diapers and swaddles set up

☐ Be ready with the alert sock

☐ Set up the kitchen

☐ Set up the rest of the house

☐ Go to the first doctor's visit

☐ Make at least one dad joke

☐ Nap and take care of myself

Chapter 9
NEW DAD, NEW LIFE

The biggest survival tip I can offer a new dad is to find more dad friends who are going through what you're going through. Your partner will be great, but they are a mom now and they will not understand what you are going through quite as well as other dads.

You shouldn't feel as though you need to only be friends with very experienced dads. Sometimes dads who have a child even younger than your own will be helpful to bounce ideas off of and talk through things with.

As you and your child continue to grow, you will get comfortable with other dads on playgrounds or in parks or wherever you decide to spend your time. Make sure you are connecting with other dads so that your social group can be filled with other supportive men who can celebrate and commiserate with you no matter what you may be going through.

Sex After the Baby:

You will really need to follow your partner's lead on this. Depending on how the birth went, it may be a long recovery period before they are physically able to have sex again. Please make sure you are patient and encouraging to your partner. Never ever pressure your partner into having sex before they are completely ready. It is best to just be patient and do what your partner feels comfortable with at a time that works well for them.

Introducing Your Baby to the Outside World:

When you feel ready to take your baby out into the world, you should take plenty of precautions to make sure everyone is safe. You will need to wear sunscreen if you live in an area with high UV rates. You will need to have plenty of warm clothes on your baby if you live in a cold climate. You should do your best to keep your baby away from sick people as their tiny immune systems are not fully developed yet.

For the first few months, you probably won't be doing too much out and about because the baby isn't developed enough to sit up on their own, crawl, walk, or do much of anything. In all likelihood, if you are going out with your baby, they are probably in a stroller or wrapped or strapped to your body.

Still, this can be a good opportunity for you to do things like visit the zoo or a museum. You can take your child somewhere new and show them animals and art that they have not seen before. You can keep a close eye on them during this time. You will not always be able to keep them so close to you, so enjoy this phase while it lasts.

Planning for Another Baby?

You have done such a good job planning for this baby, it would not be surprising if you wanted to start planning for the next. Be sure you have plenty of good conversations with your partner before you dive into pregnancy again. Take time to enjoy this new life. Most doctors suggest you wait at least a year between pregnancies, so take your time and do not rush ahead into another baby before you are ready.

Of course, things happen, and if you end up being pregnant again soon, you already have a book and now you have plenty of life experience to make sure you will be ready.

CONCLUSION

Well, you did it! You made it to the end of this book. I hope you know this is really just the beginning of the rest of your life. Things will never be the same from now on. You're a dad and you always will be for the rest of your life. It will be your number one identity, more than your career title, you are a father now. That is who you are.

And as a dad, you did a great job by getting this book, taking it to heart, and preparing as best as you can for the first phase of your child's life. You've done so much more for your child than they will know unless they end up having children of their own someday. You have taken time since the moment you found out about the pregnancy to take steps towards having a healthy pregnancy and relationship, so that this baby can come into the world in the safest and healthiest way possible.

You are already showing your partner and your baby that you are putting them first, that they mean the world to you, and that you'd do anything for them. You'd even read a book, even if you aren't the book reading type!

Seriously though, I hope you feel a sense of accomplishment for doing all of the hard things you've done over the past nine months. Everyone always talks about what the mom has gone through, and to be clear, what you've done will never hold a candle to what she's done. I mean, she created life within her body.

But that doesn't mean that you haven't done some pretty marvelous things yourself. You took the initiative to make the pregnancy go as smoothly as possible. You invested in your relationship with your partner and your future relationship with your child by doing everything you could for them during these past nine months.

Of course, no book could ever prepare you for everything, but that is a small glimpse into fatherhood as well. You could read every fatherhood book, take every parenting class, and do everything you possibly could to be ready for what that baby is going to grow up to be and there is absolutely no way you'd ever come even close to being ready for what the future holds.

Luckily, life doesn't work like that. You aren't expected to be ready for everything. You are, however, expected to respond to the little surprises in life with love and with grace. And you can be proud of being a dad who responds with love and grace. Start practicing now when they pee on you and when they're older, you'll be able to remember that they peed on you and your response was love and grace, so surely you can handle whatever they do to upset you with an equal measure of that love and grace.

On a personal note, I want to thank you. Not every dad takes the time to do what you're doing. Our children will end up being the next generation, and if your kid grows up to have the same kind of thoughtfulness that you've displayed while preparing for this pregnancy and birth, then the world that our children will share will be a better place because of them and because of you.

Even if no one else says it, I'll say it: I'm proud of you for doing what you did during this pregnancy. You're going to be a great dad!

Thank You!

This is a quick message of thanks that you picked my book from dozens of other books available for you to purchase.

Thank you for getting this and reading this all the way to the end.

Before you go, I'd like to ask a minute of your time to leave me a review on Amazon. As an indie author, every review (or star rating) matters as it helps our books become more visible on the platform thus in turn helps us reach and help more people.

Here are the links for your convenience:

Leave a review in:

US   **UK**   **CA**

GLOSSARY

☐ **Aspirator**: An apparatus for producing suction or moving or collecting materials by suction; *especially*: a hollow tubular instrument connected with a partial vacuum and used to remove fluid or tissue or foreign bodies from the body, often nasal aspirators are used with babies

☐ **Bassinet**: A baby's basketlike bed (as of wickerwork or plastic) often with a hood over one end

☐ **Custody**: Immediate charge and control (as over a ward or a suspect) exercised by a person or an authority, legal guardian of a child

☐ **Delivery**: The passing of the baby from inside of the mother to the outside world, either vaginally or through C-section; placenta is also considered delivered when it exits the woman's body as well

☐ **Doppler**: Heartbeat monitoring machine that can detect fetal heartbeats

☐ **Doula:** A person trained to provide advice, information, emotional support, and physical comfort to a mother before, during, and just after childbirth

☐ **Epidural:** An injection of a local anesthetic into the space outside the dura mater of the spinal cord in the lower back region to produce loss of sensation especially in the abdomen or pelvic region

☐ **Gestation:** The carrying of offspring in the uterus

☐ **Gestational Diabetes:** A condition characterized by an elevated level of glucose in the blood during pregnancy, typically resolving after the birth.

☐ **Group B Streptococcus:** A bacterial infection, usually harmless in adults, but can be dangerous in newborns and adults with chronic conditions, such as diabetes or liver disease. Symptoms in newborns include fever, trouble feeding, and lethargy. Adults who are immunocompromised may get a urinary tract or blood infection, or pneumonia.

☐ **Labor:** During the three stages of labor, your body will prepare for the birth of your baby (stage one), deliver the baby (stage two) and deliver the placenta (stage three). Throughout labor, the body will use contractions to dilate and efface the cervix.

☐ **Lactation:** The production and secretion of milk by the mammary glands

☐ **Meconium**: A dark greenish mass that accumulates in the bowel during fetal life and is discharged shortly after birth

☐ **Midwife**: A person who assists women in childbirth

☐ **Miscarriage**: Spontaneous expulsion of a human fetus before it is viable and especially between the 12th and 28th weeks of gestation, occurring in about 1 of every 8 pregnancies

☐ **Placenta**: The vascular organ in most mammals that joins the fetus to the maternal uterus and mediates nutrients and oxygen that the fetus receives from the mother

☐ **Postpartum**: Occurring in or being the period following childbirth

☐ **Postpartum depression**: Depression suffered by a mother following childbirth, typically arising from the combination of hormonal changes, psychological adjustment to motherhood, and fatigue

☐ **Prenatal**: Occurring, existing, performed, or used before birth

☐ **Seizmophobe**: Someone afraid of earthquakes

☐ **Self-Care**: Healthcare, whether physical, spiritual, or mental, provided by and for oneself

☐ **Stillbirth**: The birth of a dead fetus

☐ **Tdap**: A vaccine in a class of combination vaccines against three infectious diseases in humans (tetanus, diphtheria, and pertussis). The vaccine components include diphtheria and tetanus toxoids and either killed whole cells of the bacterium that causes pertussis or pertussis antigens

☐ **Trimester**: In pregnancy, a period of three months which demarcate different phases of the pregnancy

☐ **Ultrasound**: The diagnostic or therapeutic use of ultrasound and especially a noninvasive technique involving the formation of a two-dimensional image used for the examination and measurement of internal body structures and the development of the fetus in the uterus

REFERENCES

{{meta.og.title}}. (n.d.). Www.pregnancybirthbaby.org.au.
    https://www.pregnancybirthbaby.org.au/second-
    trimester
Baby Registry Checklist | buybuy BABY | buybuy BABY.
    (n.d.). Www.buybuybaby.com. Retrieved September
    6, 2022, from
    https://www.buybuybaby.com/store/registry/Registr
    yChecklist

Merriam-Webster. (2022). *Merriam-Webster Dictionary.*
    Merriam-Webster.com. https://www.merriam-
    webster.com/dictionary/

Schedule of prenatal care. (n.d.).
    https://www.uclahealth.org/obgyn/workfiles/Pregna
    ncy/Schedule_of_Prenatal_Care.pdf

The Third Trimester. (n.d.). Www.hopkinsmedicine.org.
    https://www.hopkinsmedicine.org/health/wellness-
    and-prevention/the-third-

trimester#:~:text=During%20the%20third%20trime
ster%2C%20your

National Childbirth Trust. (2019a, April 2). *Dad-to-be guide: 10 facts for the third trimester*. NCT (National Childbirth Trust). https://www.nct.org.uk/pregnancy/dads-be/dad-be-guide-10-facts-for-third-trimester

National Childbirth Trust. (2019b, May 29). *Second trimester: 10 big things to think about for dads*. NCT (National Childbirth Trust). https://www.nct.org.uk/pregnancy/dads-be/second-trimester-10-big-things-think-about-for-dads

National Childbirth Trust. (2019c, June 12). *First trimester: tips for dads to be*. NCT (National Childbirth Trust). https://www.nct.org.uk/pregnancy/dads-be/first-trimester-tips-for-dads-be